*Stephen J. Hiemstra's My Travel Through Life brings back wonderful memories of the formative times in U.S. food policies and programs, and the people involved. Those who were active in agricultural economics from the 1960s to the end of the century are reminded that this creative period saw the birth pangs, growth and refinement of food programs that are taken for granted by many today. For most of those programs, Hiemstra was present at the creation, preparing the necessary preliminary research, analyzing options, evaluating results, advising policy makers and informing important audiences. His role in the evolution of USDA's programs that now feed millions of Americans should not be understated. There is much more to learn and enjoy in this very readable journey of a very productive life."*

Dr. John E. Lee, Jr.
retired Administrator of USDA's Economic Research Service and Professor Emeritus, Mississippi State University.


*I remember my nephew Stephen as a handsome and well mannered young man. I knew he would be successful as he grew up with good Christian parents. After he married Hazel, they would always visit John and I on the farm when they came to Iowa. I normally served coffee time which included my homemade buns. I always enjoyed Stephen and Hazel, and appreciated their visits.*

Aunt Leona (Hiemstra) TerLouw
Pella, Iowa

*As we learned from Dr. Stephen J. Hiemstra, life is a journey where we travel from moment to moment, from research to education, from government to university, from discovery to discovery. As one of his first doctoral students, I caught his passion for the journey, his passion for research, his passion to live life in its fullest—it was an honor to have been his student. For me, he was a role model and a mentor that I will never forget.*

Hailin Qu, Ph.D.
Regents Professor & William E. Davis Distinguished Chair
Director of the Center for Hospitality & Tourism Research
School of Hotel and Restaurant Administration
Oklahoma State University


*Stephen Hiemstra's accomplishments are overshadowed by the care he showed as a father, husband, mentor, and colleague. His autobiography shows his journey throughout his life, how his life work touched the lives of thousands, and his contributions to his discipline, government, and organizations that he committed his professional life. Dr. Hiemstra was a brilliant thinker and problem solver, who was patient with those who didn't have his intellect. He was also a man of God, a statesman, a leader, and, more importantly, my friend.*

Dr. Carl A. Boger Jr.
Professor, Clinton L. Rappole Endowed Chair
College of Hotel and Restaurant Management
University of Houston

*Dr. Stephen Hiemstra was my advisor during my doctoral program at Purdue University and I would like to thank him for his dedication in helping me begin my own career as a hospitality researcher. He is a real gentleman who invited doctoral students to his house for dinner, a practice which I have continued with my own students.*

Dr. Woody G. Kim
Professor, Robert H. Dedman Professor of Hospitality Management
Director of Graduate Studies and of the International Center for Hospitality Research and Development
College of Business, Florida State University


*Dr. Hiemstra is a great example of the value to society (and for himself) of higher education, made possible for many through the land grant university system. His impact on society through his work at Purdue University and the United States Department of Agriculture will be long remembered.*

Dr. Neil E. Harl[1]
Charles F. Curtiss Distinguished Professor in Agriculture
Emeritus Professor of Economics , Member, Iowa Bar
Former Director, Center for International Agricultural Finance

---

1 Also see: *Appendix D: Reflections on a Career of Accomplishments by Neil E. Harl.*

OTHER BOOKS BY T2PNEUMA PUBLISHERS LLC:

*A Christian Guide to Spirituality (2014)*

*Una Guía Cristiana a la Espiritualidad (2015)*

*Life in Tension (2016)*

# MY TRAVEL THROUGH LIFE

Professor Stephen J. Hiemstra at Purdue University

# MY TRAVEL THROUGH LIFE

*Memoir of Family Life and Federal Service*

Stephen J. Hiemstra

T2Pneuma Publishers LLC
*Centreville, Virginia*

# MY TRAVEL THROUGH LIFE
Memoir of Family Life and Federal Service

© 2016 Stephen J. Hiemstra. All Rights Reserved
ISNI: 0000-0000-2990-6376

With the except of short excerpts used in articles and critical reviews, no part of this work may be reproduced, transmitted, or stored in any form whatsoever, printed or electronic, without prior written permission of the publisher.

*T2Pneuma Publishers LLC*
P.O. Box 230564, Centreville, Virginia 20120
http://www.T2Pneuma.com

The cover image is Claude Monet's Boulevard des Capucines, 1873-1874. Oil on canvas. The Nelson-Atkins Museum of Art, Kansas City, Missouri. Purchase: the Kenneth A. and Helen F. Spencer Foundation Acquisition Fund, F72-35. (http://www.Nelson-Atkins.org)

Cover and book design by SWH

Publisher's Cataloging-in-Publication (Provided by Quality Books, Inc.)

    Hiemstra, Stephen J., 1931- author.
      My travel through life : memoir of family life and
    federal service / Stephen J. Hiemstra.
      pages cm
      Includes bibliographical references.
      LCCN 2015916810
      ISBN 978-1942199038

      1. Hiemstra, Stephen J., 1931- 2. United States. Department of Agriculture—Officials and employees—Biography. 3. Agricultural economists—United States—Biography. 4. United States. Department of Agriculture—History. 5. Farms—Iowa. 6. Autobiographies. I. Title.

HD1771.5.H54A3 2016    338.1092    QBI16-900008

To my wife, Hazel, and our family, especially our four children—Stephen Wayne, Diane Sue, Karen Lee, and John David—who inspired me to do my best and to write this memoir. You are always in my thoughts.

# FOREWORD
By Rev. Dr. John E. Hiemstra[1]

In this foreword I am pleased to introduce my brother, Stephen's, memoir from the days on our family farm through his service as an economist with the U.S. Department of Agriculture.

Although I was 3 years older than my brother, Stephen was clearly the brains of the family. This became obvious when our family moved from one farm to another in March of 1936 and our mother, Gertrude, took me to enroll in the area's one room school house, Walker No. 6 of Spring Creek Township which was 3 miles south of the County Seat of Oskaloosa, Iowa and about a half mile from our new home. At the time, the school enrolled about 10 or 12 students in the eight grades offered.

After enrolling me in the third grade, the teacher turned to my brother, who was standing quietly alongside my mother, and asked: who is this? She was told that Stephen would be five years old next month in April. With a gleam in her eye and per-

---

[1] John received his bachelor's degree from Central College in Pella, Iowa, his Masters of Divinity from the New Brunswick Theological Seminary in New Brunswick, New Jersey and the Doctor of Education from Rutgers University, also in New Brunswick. He was ordained as a Minster of the Word and Sacrament by the Reformed Church in America (RCA) in 1955 and has served as a minister as well as many other denomination positions in the RCA since then. John lives with his wife, Norma in West Nyack, NY.

ceiving a bright, young man, she said: I can enroll him in kindergarten now and in the fall he can start the first grade. Stephen's academic pursuit took off from that moment forward. As the brightest of the three sons in the Hiemstra family, he went on to high school, college, and graduate school where he earned a doctorate, always at the top of his class.

One of three boys, Stephen grew up on the 160 acre farm that our father, Frank, worked hard to support us. And it was hard. When the crops failed in the depression, our Dad had to surrender his other farm east of Oskaloosa. Having lost much of his investment in the first farm, he moved to the less expensive farm in 1936 where he was able to start over and provide for his family—without the aid of tractors and power machinery—having only his own manual labor. As boys, we learned to plow and cultivate fields behind a team of horses. But we never felt poor having the example of a dedicated and hard working father and a loving mother.

Not only were we well taken care of physically, we had the gift of God's love. The focal support point for the family was the Bible and the Central Reformed Church in Oskaloosa, Iowa, a protestant church of mostly Dutch heritage members. The church was one of about 20 Dutch churches, descendants of a colony of Dutch immigrants who founded Pella (16 miles West of Oskaloosa) in 1847.

Church life had a strong influence on our family. We attended Church twice on Sundays—Sunday school and worship on Sunday mornings and worship again on Sunday evening. We also attend weekly Bible study and catechism on Saturdays. Sunday afternoons were spent reading or taking a nap, unless we were visiting our grandparents.[1]

The Christian faith deeply affected our father and our family. He prayed with us every day and urged us to maintain a deep commitment to Jesus Christ. As a youth, my father wanted to become a minister and started attending the Central Academy to pursue this dream, but family obligations forced him to drop out. So he encouraged his sons to enter the ministry, which I did—as a boy of seven or eight I took his dream as my own and studied to be ordained later as a minister in the Reformed Church in America.

This deep religious surrounding and commitment also impacted my brother, Stephen, but his faith took him in a different direction. Stephen wanted to be a farmer, like his father, but he wanted to be a more informed and educated farmer. His aca-

---

[1] Church members who only attended Sunday morning services were referred to as: *"once -ers"*.

demic bent therefore took him to enroll in Iowa State College at Ames, Iowa. But, having experienced the academic life, he never returned to the farm.

After completing a two year degree aimed at farm operation, Stephen switched to a four year program in agricultural economics. Ironically, his love for agricultural economics led him to his other love, the lovely Hazel (Billie) Deacon, who he met while attending an agricultural ecnomics conference in Guelph, Ontario, Canada. They were married during his last year at Ames. After attending the Reserved Officer Training Corps (ROTC) in college, he enlisted in the U.S. Air Force where he was commissioned as a Second Lieutenant and was sent to serve as a communications officer at a base near Seoul, Korea. After completing his miliarty service, he returned to Iowa State to complete a master's degree and, later, to the University of California in Berkley to complete a doctorate (Ph.D.) in agricultural economics.

After graduate school, in 1960 Stephen accepted a position with the in the U.S. Department of Agriculture (USDA). In USDA, he distinguished himself in research, publication, and administration. From 1960 to 1969 he wrote numerous articles for the National Food Situation (NFS), but in July of 1969, he and a colleague, Al Egbert, published a study, "*Shifting Direct Gov-*

ernment Payments from Agriculture to Poor People: Impacts on Food Consumption and Farm Income," which set the stage for the rest of his career. He soon joined the Food and Nutrition Service (FNS) where he worked on: Food Stamp Program, the Child Nutrition Programs, the School Lunch Program, the Child Care Food Service, and the Woman, Infants, and Children Program (WIC).[1] Stephen details the research and implementation done in these programs in this book.

Following his years with the FNS, Stephen served as an executive in the new Council on Wage and Price Stability created by President Jimmy Carter in October 1978 and later dissolved when President Ronald Reagan took office in 1981. At that point, Stephen returned to USDA.

In this book Stephen chronicles experiences that he had, including an invitation to an event with his family in the White House with President Carter. In 1983 Stephen retired from federal service and moved to West Lafayette, Indiana where he accepted a teaching and research position with Purdue University. There he founded and directed a doctoral program in the Department of Hospitality and Tourism Management, which was

---

[1] Stephen coined the acronym, WIC, and he was later referred to as: *"The father of the WIC program."*.

the first such program in hospitality anywhere in the world.

In addition to his professional accomplishments, Stephen remained devoted to his faith and his family. He was baptized and confirmed at the Central Reformed Church[1] in Oskaloosa, Iowa and was later ordained as an elder by the Presbyterian church, another denomination in the reformed tradition. Details of the Hiemstra family history are found in the appendices.

John Elmer

---

[1] Central Reformed Church is affiliated with the Reformed Church in America, which is found neither in the Washington DC area nor West Lafayette, Indiana, where Stephen has lived and worked since leaving Iowa. In the absernce of a reformed church, Stephen became a Presbyterian.

# PREFACE

By Stephen W. Hiemstra (Son)

*D*ad's work on this memoir spanned a period of years, starting around 2005 and running through 2012, when I came in possession of a hardcopy manuscript. In the summer of that year, I scanned copies of the manuscript for a family CD which I distributed at my parent's 60th wedding anniversary in September of that year.

Dad's writes about his life from early childhood through 1983, when he took early retirement from federal service at age 52. The Thursday night before he retired from federal service, we talked about the prospect of early retirement. The next day he filed his paperwork and said his goodbyes. On Saturday and Sunday, he played a couple rounds of golf. By the end of the following week he had found a position as associate professor in the hospitality and tourism management department at Purdue University.

The years that followed were some of his happiest and most productive. In three years, Dad was promoted to full professor and he inaugurated one of the first doctoral programs in the fields of hospitality management and tourism. Students that he advised are now leaders across the field, as endorsements to this book attest. Unfortunately, he was never personally able to chronicle his years at Purdue.

# ACKNOWLEDGMENTS

*I* would like offer thanks to everyone who assisted in preparing and editing this book, especially my brother, John D. Hiemstra.

Special thanks go to Barbara Almanza and the faculty of the School of Hospitality and Tourism Management at Purdue University who took time to reflect on Dad's contribution to their school over the period from 1983 through 1998 and who prepared an oral history on CD. Faculty members participating in the hour-long discussion were: Howard Adler, Liping Cai, Richard Ghiselli, Joseph Ismail, Shawn Jang, Xinran Lehto, Doug Nelson, and John Rousselle.

# CONTENTS

**DEDICATION** ........................................................................... v

**FOREWORD** ........................................................................ vii

**PREFACE** ............................................................................ xiii

**ACKNOWLEDGMENTS** ...................................................... xv

**ABBREVIATIONS AND ACRONYMS** ............................ xxi

## INTRODUCTION

Growing Up in Iowa ................................................................. 3

Beginnings ................................................................................. 4

Family Life ................................................................................. 5

Family Trips ............................................................................. 13

Grade School and Beyond ...................................................... 15

The Farm .................................................................................. 18

## IOWA STATE UNIVERSITY

Student Life ............................................................................. 26

Roller Skating ......................................................................... 33

Canadian Relatives ................................................................. 36

Canadian Travels .................................................................... 40

## UNITED STATES AIR FORCE

Lackland Air Force Base ........................................................ 46

Scott Air Force Base ............................................................... 49

Service in Korea ...................................................................... 51

Off Duty in Korea ................................................................... 56

## GRADUATE SCHOOL

Master's Degree ....................................................................... 64

Doctor of Philosophy ............................................................. 68

Travels in California ............................................................... 75

## ECONOMIC RESEARCH SERVICE, USDA

Marketing Economics Division ............................................ 86

Economic and Statistical Analysis Division ....................... 90

Interesting Travel ................................................................. 100

## FOOD NUTRITION SERVICE, USDA

New Assignment ................................................................... 108

Food Stamp Program .......................................................... 122

Child Nutrition Programs .................................................. 143

Child Care Food Service ..................................................... 165

Women, Infant, and Children Program ........................... 168

Personal Travel ..................................................................... 173

Mr. Hekman's Retirement .................................................. 180

New Administrator ............................................................. 182

## COUNCIL ON WAGE AND PRICE STABILITY

The FAT Division ................................................................. 190

Industry Meetings ................................................................ 197

Second and Third Years ...................................................... 202

Program Evaluation ............................................................ 204

Other Travel ........................................................................ 211

## RETURN TO THE FOOD NUTRITION SERVICE, USDA

Changing of the Guard ....................................................... 218

Other Travel ........................................................................ 230

## A SON'S REFLECTION

Family Life .......................................................................... 234

Professional Work ............................................................... 235

Purdue University ............................................................... 237

Past Time ............................................................................ 240

Faithfulness as a Churchman .............................................. 241

## APPENDIX A: FAMILY CHRONOLOGIES

Brief History of Friesland .................................................... 267

Hiemstra Family History .................................................... 269

A Brief History of Ede ........................................................ 277

Tysseling, Van Zee, and DeKock Family Histories ........... 279

Brief History of Pella, Iowa ................................................ 286

**APPENDIX B: BIOGRAPHY OF STEPHEN J. HIEMSTRA** ........................................................................ 287

**APPENDIX C: PLACES LIVED AND CHURCHES ATTENDED**

Places Lived ........................................................................ 289

Churches Attended ............................................................ 290

**APPENDIX D: REFLECTIONS ON A CAREER OF ACCOMPLISHMENTS BY NEIL E. HARL** ................... 291

# ABBREVIATIONS AND ACRONYMS

Agency for International Development (AID)
Agriculture Marketing Service (AMS)
Agricultural Research Service (ARS)
Aid to Families with Dependent Children (AFDC)

Allied Social Science Associations (ASSA)
American Agricultural Economic Association (AAEA)
American Economic Association (AEA)
American Finance Association (AFA)

American Journal of Farm Economics (AJFE)
American School Food Service Association (ASFSA)
Bachelor Officers Quarters (BOQ)
Bachelor of Science (B.S.)

Centre National Des Exposition Et Concours Agricoles (CENECA)
Child Care Foodservice Programs (CCFP)
Child Nutrition Programs (CNP)
Computer Assisted Menu Planning (CAMP)

Congressional Budget Office (CBO)
Consumer Price Index (CPI)
Contracting Officer's Representative (COR)
Council on Wage and Price Stability (CWPS)

Demilitarized Zone (DMZ)
Doctor of Philosophy (Ph.D.)
Eligibility Purchase Requirement (EPR)
Economic Research Service, USDA (ERS)

Food, Agriculture, and Trade Division (FAT)
Food Distribution Program (FDP)
Food and Nutrition Service, USDA (FNS)
Food Consumption Section of the Economic and Statistical Analysis Division (ESAD)

Fiscal Year (FY)
Food Distribution Program (FDP)
Food Stamp Program (FSP)
Future Farmers of America (FFA)

Grocery Manufacturers of America (GMA)
Gross National Product (GNP)
Household Food Consumption Survey (HFCS)
Iowa State University (ISU)

International Conference of the American Farm Economics Association (AFEA)
Marginal Propensity to Consume Food (MPC
Marketing and Transportation Situation (MTS)

National Food Situation (NFS)
National School Lunch Act (NSLA)
National School Lunch Program (NSLP)
Nutrient Standard Menu Planning (NSMP)

Nutrition and Technical Services Division (NTSD)
Nutrition and Technical Services Staff (NTSS)
Office of Economic Opportunity (OEO)
Office of Management and Budget (OMB)

Office of Price Monitoring (OPM)
Office of Policy, Planning, and Evaluation (OPPE)
Post Exchange (PX)
Program Reporting Staff (PRS)

Recommend Dietary Allowances (RDA)
Reformed Church of America (RCA)
Request for Proposals (RFP)
Reserve Office Training Corps (ROTC)

Residential Child-Care Center (RCCI)
Rest and Recuperation (R&R)
School Breakfast Program (SBP)
Social Security Insurance (SSI)

Society of Government Economists (SGE)
Special Milk Program (SMP)
Standard Industrial Code (SIC)
Television (TV)

Textured Vegetable Protein (TVP)
Transfer Income Model (TRIM)
U.S. Department of Agriculture (USDA)
Women, Infant, and Children (WIC) Program

Young Men's Christian Association (YMCA)

# INTRODUCTION

*M*y professional interests have progressed from farm production to food away from home to hotel and tourism management. As a young man, I dreamed of following my father into farming. Under the influence of the 4-H Club and Future Farmers of America (FFA), however, I realized that I wanted to becoming an educated farmer, which required attending college. Under other influences, my interest in farming shifted even further. Now, my most recent adventure as a Senior Research Fellow in Tourism Management at George Washington University is entirely outside the fields of farming, agribusiness, and food. These career shifts transgressed many educational and professional boundaries, and were far removed from my agricultural roots.

The constants in my professional life have been economic analysis and research, while the constants in my personal life have been my faith in God and a stable family life, for which I thank my parents and my wife. Without these constants and the blessings of a few favorable financial decisions, life would have been very different.

This story details my life's wandering through open doors and avoiding the closed ones, but always with prayerful consideration. Plans must sometimes change to account for new opportunities both at home and abroad. Still, I learned early on that variety is the spice of life.

In fact, my career was full of such spice. I served in the U.S. Air Force, including a year in Korea. After completing my military service, I worked in two different agencies in the the U.S. Department of Agriculture, the Economic Research Service (ERS) and the Food and Nutrition Service (FNS). While at FNS, I was also assigned for two years at the Council on Wage and Price Stability (CWPS) in the Office of the President and had my picture taken in the Oval Office with then President Jimmy Carter. Following my federal retirement, I started an entirely new career as a professor at Purdue University, in West Lafayette, Indiana.

While I am now retired from Purdue and living in Northern Virginia, a bit down the road from Iowa, I never forgot my father's legacy or the farm that we worked together so long ago, as I hope you will agree having read the pages that follow.

# GROWING UP IN IOWA

Beginnings

Family Life

Family Trips

Grade School and Beyond

The Farm

## Beginnings

*I* was born in Iowa on April 17, 1931, the second of three sons. My older brother, John Elmer was born June 21, 1928 and my younger brother, David Lee was born August 27, 1932.[1] We lived on a farm about four miles south of Oskaloosa, the county seat of Mahaska County.

Oskaloosa, an Indian name,[2] is a typical small mid-western town with a stable population of 10,000—then and now—and prominent red-brick court house opposite the town square. The town square has a park with a statue of Chief Mahaska and an elevated band-shell at its center.

As I remember it, summer band concerts on the square were the focal point of social life on Saturday evenings. Everyone came to town for the concerts—some came to sit and listen to the band; others came to show off their new cars by driving around the square. I continued to live near Oskaloosa on the farm through my college years and afterwards I visited it as often as time allowed.

---

[1] David passed away December 9, 1995 at age 63 from pancreatic cancer and is buried in Cedar Rapids, Iowa, where he lived most of his adult life. David attended Kenwood Park Presbyterian Church and is buried in Cedar Memorial Park Cemetery both in Cedar Rapids, Iowa.
[2] https://en.wikipedia.org/wiki/Oskaloosa,_Iowa.

## Family Life

My father, Frank Henry Hiemstra, was born on August 30, 1898 near Otley, Iowa, about 5 miles north and west of Pella on state road 63. My mother, Gertrude Henrietta DeKock, was born June 30, 1906, near Leighton about halfway between Oskaloosa and Pella on state road 63. Dad and mom were married on December 17, 1925 and were married for 74 years when she died at the age of 93 on April 22, 1999. Dad died the following year at the age of 102 on October 4, 2000.[1]

Mom told us kids that you have to eat a pint of dirt sometime during your life so don't be too fussy about a little dirt. My mother was herself always immaculately clean. She also liked to run the vacuum cleaner early in the morning before us kids were out of bed. She was an early riser, like 5:00 am, especially on *"washday,"* which was Monday, and I mean every Monday.

Dave and I both developed a case of whooping cough when we were young. We whooped all one winter, and even later when we would get a cold we would sometimes start whooping which is a very distinctive, repetitive cough. Most of you have probably never heard of this disease. I remember getting the measles, both red measles and the 3-day, German variety but I

---
[1] Gertrude died having suffered from Alzheimer's disease for many years. Frank died from complications due to surgery for a blocked intestine.

never got anything really serious like diphtheria or scarlet fever that other people occasionally would get.

For those diseases, families would be quarantined in their houses for a few weeks. I think my brother John had smallpox but it was before Dave and I were born so we did not catch it from him; I'm not sure if my parents had it or not.

I remember one incident from my childhood that was not very pleasant. I don't know what I was doing at the time, but somehow several bees got up the pant leg of my bib overalls (we did not wear jeans) and stung me many times. My parents rushed me to the doctor and he gave me some medication and calmed me down. I remember that it hurt a lot at first, but I did not have a severe reaction to the stings so I survived. Maybe it gave me immunity to bee stings. I understand that kids that grow up on farms have fewer allergy problems than kids who live a more sheltered life in town because they grow up with pollen, rag weeds, etc., from which they gain immunity.

I'm not sure that helped us kids though because my brother Dave had a severe case of asthma when he was young and almost died from it. Mother and Dad tried various poultices and hot packs on his chest but nothing seemed to help. Finally, the doctors told us to give him plenty of fresh air, and that seemed to cure him. Of course, that was before the days of penicillin. Ever after, we had lots of fresh air in our bedroom, which I shared with Dave.

I do remember getting one serious disease, mumps, but not when I was a kid. I got it from Diane Sue who brought it home from nursery school when we lived in Lanham, Maryland about 1961. I was deliriously sick with it having a temperature of about 104 which is bad for adults. I took baths in ice water to get the temperature down. It lasted about two weeks. I apparently had no lasting effects from it; mumps can cause sterility in men but that was before John David and Karen Lee were born so apparently it did not affect me. They don't know how closely they came to never being born.

Pella, which was 16 miles north and west of Oskaloosa, was founded by a community of immigrant Dutch people about 1850. My mother was fond of telling us that her grandmother was the first child born in Pella after the settlement was established. My father's family arrived in Pella about the same time and they were also from Holland[2]. As a result, I am a purebred Dutchman even though I never learned to speak the language. I later fit right in when walking down the street in Amsterdam.

My father (but not my mother) could understand and

---
2 See appendix A for my family chronology.

speak Dutch because his parents spoke it at home till he was five years old. But, Dad never tried to teach us the language. He felt that since we were Americans we should be Americanized and speak English. That was not true of several of our relatives who harbored more inclination to hold onto their heritage. In later years, I wished that Dad had at least taught us the basics of Dutch but I am supportive of his reasoning that we should adjust to our community. Just the fact that Dad and Mother had moved near Oskaloosa and away from Pella gave us a whole different outlook on life from that of many of our relatives.

Pella, the home of nationally-advertised *Pella Windows* (in earlier years called simply the Rollscreen), remains to this day a settlement of Dutch people. Pella was founded about 1850 and named for an ancient city founded in the fourth century B.C. east of the Jordan River where Christians sought refuge during the Jewish revolt from Rome in the period A.D. 66 to 70[3]. It is the location of Central College, a church supported, liberal arts school founded by the Reformed Church of America (RCA). My brother, John, graduated from Central College and went on to

---

[3] The revolt left Jerusalem devastated in A.D. 70. Some scholars believe that Christians fled to Pella in response to the prophesy of Jesus in Matthew 24:16. It is also believed that lack of Christian support for the Jewish revolt was the political basis for the separation of Christian and Jewish faiths.

become an RCA pastor.

Every year, Pella celebrated *"Tulip Time"* for several days, around about May 10, and they still do. They commemorate the Dutch heritage by wearing Dutch costumes, including wooden shoes, in daily parades and washing the streets. The streets are still lined with tulips every spring and the town now sports a new development that includes a block-long canal, a huge windmill, and neighboring streets with houses that mimic the classic styles of those in Holland. Tulip Time draws growing numbers of Dutch people and their friends and families from long distances. Pella joins Holland, Michigan and Orange County, Iowa in hosting such celebrations.

Mother and Dad both came from large families, of eight and 11, respectively. The families were close knit and most remained near the Pella or Leighton areas. Most of my many cousins still live there although several are now scattered around the country. Like my own parents, most of their brothers and sisters also lived long lives; all of them lived into their 70s and many into their 90s. However, my father still holds the record for longevity. At my current age of 74 (2005), I currently have two aunts on my father's side and one aunt and one uncle on my Mother's side who are still living.

Religion played an important role in my family's life, both my immediate family and most of my parent's brothers and sisters. We grew up in the RCA which is often tagged with the misnomer of the Dutch Reformed Church. We had one such church[4] in Oskaloosa and there were three of them in Pella. I joined the church by profession of faith when I was in high school. There was never any question what we would do on Sunday mornings. We always went to church and Sunday school. In the afternoons, we often went to visit one or both grandparents who both lived in Pella. But, during the busy farming seasons, we took naps on Sunday afternoons.

My father liked to talk about his growing up years near Otley, a few miles west of Pella. Being the oldest son in the family, he quit school at about the third grade to help his father farm. They farmed with horses and drove a horse and buggy to town. They never had a car until my father was 19 years old, which was in 1917 when they bought a *"Model T"* Ford. His father never learned to drive a car but his mother did. Dad bought his own Model T as soon as he could afford to pay the few hundred dollars that they cost at that time.

Dad farmed with his father till he was 21 years old, which

---
4 Central Reformed Church, Oskaloosa, Iowa

was the custom at the time. Then, he bought three horses and rented an 80-acre farm nearby. At that time he went to farm with his Grandmother for a year. Then, his sister Emma needed help with her farm because her husband had died, so he lived with his sister and farmed her farm for two years until he got married.

Mother and Dad were married on December 7, 1925. Emma moved to town at that time and Mother and Dad continued to farm her farm, which was near Otley. In 1928, my folks bought a farm east of Oskaloosa.

With the onset of the depression in 1929, it was a bad time to go into debt, Times were tough in the early 1930s, with extremely low prices (like 10 cents for a bushel of corn) and then back-to-back years of extreme drought and hordes of grasshoppers, which I vaguely remember. Dad said that coal was more expensive to buy than the money he could get for his corn during some of these years. Many farmers burned their corn for heat, Dad told me once. But, he was against the idea on principle because many people were going hungry in the towns. I wonder now what he would think of making ethanol out of corn.

With the depression, my Dad could not keep up his mortgage payments and he gave up the farm to his creditors and rented it back for a few years. In 1936, he scraped together enough money to buy another farm south of Oskaloosa, 160 acres for about $10,000. One of my earliest memories (I was 5 years old) was of the day that we moved to the new farm and I began to go to school. Dad and Mother lived on that farm for 38 years until he retired from farming and moved to town at about age 75.

Mother quit school about the fourth grade, but she was not happy about dropping out. She stayed home to help care for her several younger sisters and brothers. When several of them later completed high school, she felt deprived.

Mother's experience staying home may have motivated her to support me when I wanted to go to college. I was one of the first—if not the first—of our close relatives to attend college.

### Family Trips

*M*y parents never did much traveling, in part, because my father did not seem interested in it unless we were going to see some relatives at a distance. Most of our immediate relatives lived within 30 miles of us. We had one exception: Dad's sister, Mabel and her husband Clifford DeJong. They left Oskaloosa and moved to Chicago because the U.S. Post Office transferred him to Chicago for a few years. When I was about 10 years old, we decided we should go visit them in Chicago. We drove our Model A Ford there and had a great time visiting the Chicago zoo and other attractions, such as the Buckingham fountain located in a park on Grant Street near Lake Michigan. I was much impressed both by the zoo and by this fountain which changed colors at night. Not many years ago, I noticed that the fountain is still there. And the zoo is still a great zoo.

The only other trip I remember taking was a trip with my mother and brother Dave to Denver when I was in high school. Dad did not want to go along, and I don't think John did either. Dad did not care for mountains—he thought a good field of corn was more impressive. We saw the usual attractions and marveled at the mountains and other sites near Denver: Pikes Peak, Garden of the Gods, Seven Falls, and Red Rock, a natural amphitheater near Denver. We drove up Pikes Peak in our 1939 Chevrolet. I was driving and it was the highlight of the trip. Many cars had troubles and were stopped along the road with their radiators boiling over, but we managed ok. I think we stopped occasionally to let the engine cool. We stayed in a motel, which was perhaps a first for us. We drove home late at night and at one point driving across Nebraska we had a disagreement about the direction we were driving; there were no interstates at that time, the road signs were infrequent, and the road was desolate. We stopped the car in the middle of nowhere and looked for the North Star, which we found. It confirmed that we were headed east and toward Iowa.

The next trip out of state that I remember taking with the family was a drive to Kansas to visit my brother, Dave, who had enlisted in the Army and was inducted at Fort Riley. I was in college at Iowa State at that time (about 1952). Later, we drove to Indianapolis to visit Dave when he was stationed there.

### Grade School and Beyond

My brothers and I attended a one-room school with a single teacher that had 10-12 students as long as I attended. The school was about a half mile from home and we walked it every day when the weather was fit, and sometimes not so fit. Two others students, Byron and Garlyn Engelhoven, lived on a farm beyond ours, so we normally walked together. There were four students in my class, which made it the largest class in the school. When I started school, I was the only one in my class. I was moved up one grade to be with a larger class after consultation with the county superintendent who came out to talk to the teacher and me about it. As a result, I graduated from high school just one month after reaching 17 years of age.

We had some good grade school teachers. One that stands out in my mind was Adeline Moore, who stimulated me to do a lot of reading outside of class, reading science and biology books that greatly influenced me in my interest in education. One of my three classmates, Jack Thorp, became a specialized medical doctor, who now lives in San Francisco. I met him at our 50th high school graduation anniversary after not seeing him since high school. Our other two classmates did not even go to high school. Go figure.

We had no middle schools in Iowa. Elementary school contained eight grades and high school contained 9th through the 12th grade. I went to high school in Oskaloosa. We had no school buses so we had to furnish our own transportation. At age 14, I obtained a school permit to drive a car, which meant that I could drive only to and from high school or with an adult until age 16. I had learned to drive at about age 12, by driving a tractor and our Model A Ford around the farm. My older brother, John, was two grades ahead and a younger brother, Dave, was two grades behind me, so I always had someone to accompany me to high school. We carried sack lunches to high school, as we did to grade school. I don't remember if the high school even had a cafeteria; the kids in town usually went home for lunch. I usually went to the Young Men's Christian Association (YMCA), wolfed down my lunch, and played basketball or swam during the lunch period.

In high school, I developed quite an interest in basketball. Our Future Farmers of America (FFA) class sponsored basketball teams with neighboring towns' teams. At home we played at the YMCA, and we had a good coach, Max Franklin. Max's younger sister, Norma, later married my brother, John. Leonard,

Norma's younger brother, was also on the team. I played forward or center because I had long arms for my height. Ken Bailey, another guy on the team, was taller than me but I often could outjump him. Our team did quite well and my senior year I often scored about 20 points per game. I often regretted not being able to play basketball till I got to high school. I would like to have played on the varsity team.

I did quite well academically in high school graduating 7th in a class of 154. I even studied Latin for one semester because I was told it would help in learning good English. Perhaps it helped. At least it made one aware of verb conjugations that we take for granted in English. I also studied algebra, which I enjoyed, and chemistry that I found fascinating, probably because we had an unusually fine instructor. But, perhaps the most practical course I took in high school was a semester of typing. I didn't plan to be a secretary, like most of the members of the class, but I knew that I wanted to go to college and figured that it would help me type term papers. I later typed my Ph.D. dissertation on an old Underwood, manual typewriter.

### The Farm

I grew up on a farm of 160 acres. It did not seem so small when I was young because 160 acres was about all that my Dad could handle with horses. He was slow to mechanize the operation and he did not seem to care about increasing the size of the business when most farmers were moving in that direction to make it more efficient.

He was more concerned with being self-sufficient and loathed going into debt to buy new machinery or anything else. It reflected his reaction to the hard times of the depression during the 1930s.

I loved farm animals and caring for them. This included helping Dad milk the cows (by hand) in the evenings. Dad did it himself in the mornings. We always had several beef cattle, some of which we raised as calves but mostly bought at Oskaloosa's sale barn. We fattened the calves on corn and soybean meal. We also raised quite a few hogs that farrowed (gave birth, for you city folks) little pigs and raised them to market weight of about 200-220 pounds and then sold them.

We also always raised chickens. We usually bought female baby chicks when they were a couple days old and raised them to lay eggs. But, in the early days we had an incubator in the basement in which we would place fertilized eggs and keep them warm for a few weeks until the chicks would hatch. As boys, we really liked to see them come out of their eggs. Raising our own chicks was rather inefficient because we wanted to raise only the female chicks to become laying hens. The Leghorn roosters are skinny when grown so they are not as good for eating as the more meaty breeds intended to be eaten as broilers. Leghorns, which we raised, are best at laying eggs.

Our Mother raised a lot of broiler chickens every year too. She dressed and sold a lot of them privately in town. Of course, we ate a lot of them too. I often got the job of cutting off their heads. My brother Dave helped Mother a lot with the chickens but he was a little squeamish about cutting their heads off. I think our Mother's favorite meal was chicken and noodles. We also commonly had fried chicken for Sunday dinner, which was a treat in those days.

Dad farmed with horses till 1941 when I was 10 years old. I remember driving a team of horses cutting hay and cultivating corn one row at a time. We pitched hay onto a wagon by hand, tramped down by a kid on the wagon. It was then put into the barn loose with a big fork pulled by a long rope hitched to a horse on the other side of the barn. The horse pulled the loaded fork up to the track in the barn and part way down the hayloft. I often led that horse. In later years, Dad bought a hay bailer and did it the easy way, but I was no longer at home. We also milked 6-8 cows by hand every day and picked corn by hand, throwing the ears into a wagon with a backboard to divert the corn into the wagon. During corn-picking season, we picked a wagon load of corn before going to school in the morning.

Our Dad commonly would kill and dress a hog every winter. I remember helping him with the job about when I was in high school, and it was a very messy job. We would take some of the meat to the freezer locker in town for storage and have the ham smoked. He often also took one of his calves to the locker for slaughtering and storage.

The most unpleasant job on the farm was cleaning the manure out of the barn and the henhouse each spring. The hen house was the worst because of the very unpleasant smell and it had to be carried out of the hen house, forkful by forkful. We loaded it into a wagon with a manure fork, hauled it to a field, and unloaded it by hand. In later years, Dad bought a manure spreader and we thought we really had it easy. Dad did not buy any commercial fertilizer when we were young.

The manure that we spread was the only fertilizer the

crops received. Of course, in those days, Dad and everyone else grew a four or five-year rotation of crops which included one year of corn, followed by a year of oats that contained clover or alfalfa seed which the following year would be cut for hay. The clover and alfalfa would return some nitrogen to the soil that would be there to fertilize corn the following year. If alfalfa were planted it would be left for a second year of hay.

We had a pony named Black Beauty, with a white spot on her forehead, which us boys enjoyed riding. She could really gallop down the road. For several years, I raised white rabbits when I was young. I built a nice hutch for that purpose and raised a lot of rabbits. I would dress them and sell the meat to a buyer in town. I also tried to trap some animals, like muskrats, to sell the hides but was not very successful at it. But, I enjoyed getting out and tramping around the farm, especially in the winter.

I had a BB gun at an early age and enjoyed shooting at sparrows and pigeons that were a nuisance around the farm. We also occasionally would catch pigeons up in our barn where they congregated. My Dad would do that by climbing up on a tall ladder at night while shining a flashlight in their eyes. We would sell them in Pella for eating but mostly Dad wanted to get them out of the barn where they were very messy.

We had a lot of snow every winter when I was young. I remember many problems that it caused because it would block the road for days following a big storm. The snowplow eventually would come but if we wanted out before then, Dad and us kids would shovel it out by hand for about a half mile. I remember occasional snowdrifts that were as high as the fence around the yard. We could walk on the drifts over the fence, which I thought was cool.

When I was a little older, I bought a 22-caliber rifle (which I still have) and loved to go hunting for squirrels and rabbits, which we skinned and ate. I remember once shooting seven rabbits on one successful trip and carrying them all home at one time. I had no bag to carry them in so it was difficult carrying them plus my rifle.

Until 1941, we had no electricity and no indoor plumbing. The breakthrough came when Dad was paid a few hundred dollars to allow the county to close beyond our house a road running through his farm. As a part of this agreement, I believe, the electric line was brought to our house.

This change, which also benefited us by giving us a little more land to farm but we were then at the end of the road. It required us to pick up our mail nearly a half-mile from home, but later it was brought closer.

Even so, I liked farming and planned to spend my life doing it; I was the only one of us boys with this interest. When I was a teenager, Dad let us boys raise our own pigs and a few calves. I joined the 4-H Club and showed pigs and a few calves at the county fair, which was the highlight of the year for me. I still have a lot of blue and red ribbons from the Mahaska County Fair. I even once took some pigs to the State Fair in Des Moines and also learned how to judge livestock.

That was great fun, rather profitable, and a way to meet a lot of interesting people. I became a county officer in the 4-H Club; my first real girlfriend was a fellow officer. I earned enough money from raising animals to pay my way through Iowa State College[1]. My plans were to go to college and learn to farm the scientific way.

---

1 It is now called Iowa State University (ISU).

# IOWA STATE UNIVERSITY

Student Life

Roller Skating

Canadian Relatives

Canadian Travels

## Student Life

During my first two years at Iowa State, in Ames, Iowa, I lived in the men's dormitories. I shared a room at Hughes Hall the first year with my good friend, Dale Hoover, who also was from Oskaloosa. Dale and I had been in 4-H together and shared an interest in agriculture. After the first year, he joined Farmhouse Fraternity and I moved to Friley Hall where I shared a room with two other students. We had a triple decker bed, and I slept on the top deck.

I always worked while in college to defray some of my expenses, which primarily consisted of living expenses. Tuition costs themselves were quite low. The registration fee[1] was about $45 per quarter when I was there, and there were three quarters per year.

During the first two years, I served food in the cafeteria at Friley Hall to pay for my meals. The second year, I sprained my left ankle rather badly while playing basketball, which put me in the college hospital for two days. One enjoyable thing about Friley Hall was that it overlooked Lake Lavern. In the winter, the small lake froze over and was used for ice skating. I bought a pair of skates and learned to ice skate in my spare time.

Friley Hall was also near the Memorial Union. It regular-

---
1 It was not called tuition back then.

ly hosted big name dance bands on Saturday nights that I seldom missed.

My first two years at Iowa State were devoted to very practical courses related to farming. I learned how to balance rations for cattle and hogs, studied genetics of animals and hybridization of corn. I also learned how to manage crop rotations and determine proper fertilizer applications, something about the attributes of various soil types, and how to go about determining the value of farmland. I took an interesting course in production of dairy products in which I learned how to make ice cream and cheese. But, after seeing blue cheese being produced by a thick, ugly mold, it was a long time before I could eat it. I also learned how to prune grapes. That came in handy at my home on the fall. We had planted several grape vines a few years earlier and they grew fine, but they produced a lot more grapes after I learned how to prune them properly in my horticulture class.

I earned a two-year, Farm Operations Certificate from Iowa State in June 1952 and I planned to make a career of farming. But, my farming career was short-lived. By early 1953, with the Korean War in full swing, it looked as if I would be drafted soon. Also, my farming career was not working out the way I had expected. Dad's farm was too small to employ both of us. We had tried unsuccessfully to rent more land.

I spent most of my time that year working as a carpenter and mixing mortar for cement block/brick laying for Sparks Construction at $1.00 per hour, mostly helping to build Central Reformed Church in Oskaloosa, where we were members. I also helped to raise the aluminum steeple on the church with three other workers. We did it by each of us standing on the four corners of the platform on which it stands and raising it by hand after it had been assembled in the middle of that platform. It was made of aluminum and was not heavy. Later, I worked for my Uncle, John Van Zuuk, helping him build a barn and also a small brick addition to the Reformed Church in Leighton. These jobs taught me to work with my hands which I put to use in later life, but I did not view them as a promising career.

I visited Iowa State in early February 1951, to visit with old friends. Professor Bill Thompson, one of my favorite professors who I visited, told me that if I would return to Iowa State to finish a 4-year program and took Reserved Officers Training Corp (ROTC) that I could get a commission in the army along with my B.S. degree. I had done very well with my grades and had been offered a scholarship to study agricultural economics, which I had earlier declined. I had taken the basic agricultural economics courses which I enjoyed very much, and realized that I likely could get a much better job with that degree than by farming. Thompson strongly encouraged me to return to school immediately (entering late in the quarter), and enroll in Army ROTC which I did.

When I returned to Iowa State as a junior, I immediately joined Farmhouse Fraternity with the help of my friend Dale Hoover who had joined earlier. I also had good grades which is a requisite for getting into Farmhouse. They had the reputation of always leading the "Greeks" in having the highest grade point averages for the year, which they still maintain to this day. My GPA exceeded 3.0 (on a 4.0 scale) and as a result as a senior was inducted into Alpha Zeta and Phi Kappa Phi (the counterpart of Phi Beta Kappa at Iowa State), both of which are academic honorary societies.

Living at Farmhouse, I soon took a job as a waiter for the nearby Kappa Alpha Theta sorority to pay for my meals. This job as well as working in the cafeteria at Friley Hall gave me good experience for my final career of hospitality and tourism management at Purdue University. I enjoyed fraternity life, and made a lot of good friends as a result. However, it could get a little frustrating going through their initiation, particularly as a junior, and abiding by all of their rules.

But, they regularly had dances and exchanges with the sororities located nearby. I actually lived at Farmhouse only one and a half years so did not get as involved in their activities as those that lived there for four years.

My second two years were very different from the first two. I transferred my credits to major in agricultural economics. Professor Ray Beneke became my advisor because his specialization was marketing within agricultural economics, which was my primary interest. I learned that the economics of agriculture had become highly quantitative and mathematical. This approach did not bother me because I always had done well in math, algebra, and accounting. We had a fine Department of Agricultural Economics with several nationally known professors, such as Earl Heady, a leader in Farm Production, and William Murray, head of the department and an expert in farm appraisal.

Army ROTC at Iowa State was focused on artillery, that is, learning mostly how to shoot 155 mm canons and direct their firepower. I was told that it was normally a Second Lieutenant's job to be forward observers and radio back to those shooting the guns how to make adjustments to hit their targets. That job did not appeal to me, so I soon transferred to the Air Force. I could never become a pilot because of the medical requirement for perfect vision that I did not possess. But, I learned that there were many other jobs for lieutenants that don't fly, such as becoming supply officers.

I enjoyed Air Force ROTC. Our classes were focused on teaching us how airplanes fly, the logistics of how the Air Force was organized and maintained, and the management principles of command.

I also joined Pershing Rifles, a crack drill team that competes with neighboring states schools in drill competitions, even though it is under the auspices of the Air Force. I enjoyed this activity and rose to be the executive officer (second in command) of our unit during my senior year. We traveled to drill competitions in some neighboring states by flying in the Iowa National Guard airplanes (C-47s). I recall visits to Ohio State University at Columbus, and the University of Wisconsin at Madison. At Ohio State, I had the good fortune of being paired up with the local homecoming queen to escort her to their homecoming dance. That was almost too much for an Iowa farm boy. Because of my work with Pershing Rifles, I was later inducted into Scabbard and Blade, the military honorary society at Iowa State. Many times,

I volunteered to serve in the color guard at the football games.

Pershing Rifles also drilled each spring in the VEISHEA[2] Parade at Iowa State in which I regularly participated, along with many floats. VEISHEA was a highlight celebration at Iowa State which featured inviting family and friends to Ames to demonstrate the activities of the College.

---

2 VEISHEA stands for Veterinary, Engineering, Industrial Science, Home Economics and Agriculture, which were the schools when it was first organized in 1922..

## Roller Skating

During the summer of 1951, I was offered the opportunity to attend an International Conference of the American Farm Economics Association (AFEA) to be held at the Ontario Agricultural College[1] at Guelph, Ontario Canada. A carload of professors was going. They offered me a ride so the trip would not cost me much and it sounded like an interesting experience. That turned out to be an understatement. I learned a lot at the conference, and I was voted the Secretary-Treasurer of the Student Section of AFEA.

However, the most memorable part of the trip was the extracurricular activities. I met a hometown girl named Hazel Fern (Billie) Deacon while skipping the conference banquet. We were both skating at the local skating rink when we met. I had had a couple girlfriends in high school and dated regularly in college but none of them compared well with this lassie.

I returned to Canada over Christmas vacation that winter and met Hazel at Niagara Falls near where she was working at the time in Hamilton, Ontario. We became engaged before I returned home. Hazel came to Iowa during the summer of 1952 to meet my family. We had a hard time getting her permanent residency with a green card but it finally worked out. She joined

1 It is now called the University of Guelph.

me in Red Oak, Iowa where I had a summer job as a real estate appraiser for Doane's Agriculture Service. I learned a lot on that job. Actually, it was the first professional job that I had, and I was paid the princely sum of $330 per month. I considered going into the real estate appraisal business full time after I had graduated and returned to Ames, but never followed up.

After spending the summer together, Hazel and I decided to get married before returning to Ames in the fall to finish my Bachelor of Science degree. My wife and I were married in Central Reformed Church in Oskaloosa on September 13, shortly before the school year began. My mother did most of the preparations. Hazel's Dad, Richard Henry Deacon, her brother, Richard W. (Dick), and his wife, Laura, came from Canada for the celebration. My friend, Marvin Smith, was best man.

At Ames, we lived in a two-room, upstairs apartment on Lincoln Way Avenue in the downtown part of Ames. We had to share a bathroom with the landlady but the rent was only $40 per month. Hazel worked in a restaurant a couple blocks away. Graduation was delayed an extra quarter because of my transfer to Air Force ROTC. Still, I graduated in March 1953 at the top of my class in agricultural economics and was commissioned as

Second Lieutenant in the Air Force.

## Canadian Relatives

Hazel's dad, Richard Henry Deacon, was an interesting person. He lived at 123 Grange Street in Guelph, Ontario, with several of his children. When I met him, he was running the boiler plant at the Ontario Agricultural College where I first met Hazel. He was a self-educated person, having taught himself mathematics, algebra, and enough engineering to run the boiler plant at the College. He spent most of his life working at that plant which he delighted in showing me when I met him. It was quite an impressive operation. I'm not sure how much formal education he actually had. He also had a lot of interest in local politics. Not that he ever worked as a politician, but he loved to tell me about all the problems with the ones who did. He died in his early 80s of a heart attack. He smoked his entire life, but quit *"cold-turkey"* when the doctor told him he would die if he didn't stop. He lived several years after that.

My wife's mother, Marietta (Salter) Deacon, died when Hazel was about age 11[1], so I never met her. She died with stomach cancer and was buried in Wingham, a small town about an hour's drive northwest from Guelph, where Hazel's mother and father had both grown up.

Her older brother Richard (Dick) W. Deacon had mar-

---
1 Her tombstone reads Marietta Salter, 1902 to 1943.

ried Laura before I met them. They had five children: (1) Sharron Begg who lives in Guelph with her four children. (2) Fred was divorced, but has two children, and now lives with a new wife in Echo Bay, Ontario, near Sault Ste. Marie. (3) Georgia Kreager married Don, who is deceased, and they have three children; (4) Brenda Stapleton who is divorced and has two children; they live in Guelph. (5) Roger was married to Gail but died of lung cancer in 2007. They had three children who also live in Guelph.

Dick for most of his life worked in a factory doing metal manufacturing of various kinds, and became President of his union. He was an active Mason and worked himself up to a high rank. Laura became a realtor, but died years ago of a brain aneurysm. Dick and Laura lived in the family home with his father at 123 Grange Street, Guelph, where Hazel spent her entire childhood. When her father died, Dick inherited the house, and continued to live there after his wife died. He loves golf and square dancing, doesn't smoke, and is now in his 80s living with Brenda.

Hazel had two older sisters, Frances and Marietta. Frances married Sammy and they lived for many years in Grimsby, a small town between Hamilton and Niagara Falls. They had a daughter, Sue, who married Eric Hopkiss, a school teacher and principal. They have two boys. Eric plays a saxophone in a band,

and has done so for many years. After Sammy died, while shoveling snow, Frances married a second time and moved to Alberta for a number of years. After her husband died, she moved back to live with Eric and Sue for a few years. She died in 2005.

Marietta married Ben Stuart and they had three children, Ben, [Brian], and Bonnie. They lived in Niagara Falls for several years before moving to Nova Scotia where they had grown up. When Ben died, Marietta moved back to Niagara Falls with her children where she later died of a heart attack. Ben and his sister are married and now have families of their own, living in the Niagara Falls area.

She has another older brother, George, who was a cab driver in Guelph when I first met him. He later moved to Niagara Falls, Canada, and lived there for many years, just up the hill from the Falls. He worked part-time and lived above a restaurant with a friend, Gwen, who worked as a waitress for many years. She died a few years ago. He is now living in a nursing home. Hazel also had a younger brother, Leslie, who died in a car head-on collision with a truck in 1963 at the age of 22. He had recently returned after completing a tour in Germany with the Canadian army.

Hazel also had two younger sisters, Loraine and Judy,

whom she helped care for after her mother died.

Loraine later married Wally Baker, a potato chip salesman when I knew him. They lived in Guelph for several years. They had five children: Wally Jr., Laura Lynn, Leslie Ann, Gene, and D'Arcey. When the marriage did not work out, she and her children moved to Ajax, near Toronto where she still lives. She had been an alcoholic when married to Wally Baker. When she moved to Toronto she gave up drinking and because a devote Christian.

Judy was the youngest member of the Deacon family. She married Melvin Kopperson and had a son Jeffrey. They bought a new house in the country North of Guelph, and lived there a few years. Then, she divorced Mel and they sold their house. But, they remained good friends till she died in 2001, right after September 11. She died right at the time that my daughter Karen's son, Alex Reed, was born. (We missed the funeral because we were committed to go to Florida to be with Karen at that time). Judy died in her 50s of muscular dystrophy. Jeffrey now has a family of his own.

## Canadian Travels

Over the years, we have tried to go back to Canada every couple years to see her family. Her Dad would then often drive with us to Wingham to visit some of the relatives. Aunt Helen and Uncle Charlie Searle were among the favorite relatives to visit. They lived in Kincardine which is a little farther north and west on the shores of Lake Huron. The last time we visited them, they told us that Charlie was one of the grandsons of Queen Victoria in England. They had not stayed in touch with the family and this was news to Hazel; they certainly did not live like royalty. They had two sons, one of whom lived at home. The other son was married and had a family in the area. This was the last time we saw Helen and Charlie. They were both ailing at the time, and both died a few years later.

We have done some touring in Canada, but not a lot until recently. Once from Kincardine we drove north and east to Owen Sound on Georgia Bay. That is a fishing village but apparently the fishing had deteriorated. The lower part of Ontario is a good agricultural area, rather similar to Michigan. They even grow tobacco in southern Ontario, which seemed strange to me since it is so far north. Apparently, the weather is moderated by the lake effects; they are nearly surrounded by three of the Great

Lakes. They also grow a lot of grapes, apples, and other fruits between Hamilton and Niagara Falls, near where Eric and Sue live.

At the time of the World's Fair in Montreal, probably in the 1960s, we drove with the family to Ottawa, the capital of Canada. We toured the area, witnessed the impressive changing of the guard at the capital, and then drove on to Montreal. We spent about one week at the Fair where we stayed at a nearby campsite, despite the rain all week. We drove up to Quebec one day to see the French people and their lovely city, and then returned to Montreal. We were quite impressed with the huge exhibits at the World's Fair. We did run into an old college friend of ours from Connecticut one day, along with his wife, who we saw cutting into one of the long lines to enter an exhibit. They were embarrassed when they saw us but we had a good laugh about it. We spent the rest of that pleasant day with them.

Much later, in 2003, we took a lovely Grand Circle guided tour of British Columbia by bus. We flew to Seattle a couple days ahead of the tour, and spent some time touring Seattle, which we had not visited previously. We visited Pikes Market and the Seattle Aquarium, among other things. The tour itself first took us east to the Grand Coulee Dam and on to Glacier National Park. There we drove east up the "Rising to the Sun" highway to the Logan Pass visitor center. It was late June, but there were still large drifts of snow near there. From Glacier, we drove north into Canada. Near Banff, we saw a herd of mountain goats and two or three black bears along the road. Banff itself is a lovely resort ringed by lofty mountain peaks and features the Banff Spring Hotel. From there, we visited the beautiful Moraine Lake, Chateau Lake Louise, and the Columbia Ice Fields on the way to Jasper. We took an excursion onto the Athabasca Glacier which gave us a close-up look and chance to walk on the ice. Leaving the Ice Fields, we saw a Grisly Bear walking amicably along the highway on the edge of the forest. We also saw a lot of elk around Jasper. On our way to Vancouver, we stopped by "Hells Gate" on the Frazer River.

We toured Vancouver which is a beautiful city, including the Capilano suspension bridge. Then, we spent one day touring Victoria Island and its renowned Butchart Gardens, before returning to Seattle for our flight home.

In June 2004, we drove up through Maine to Canada, stopping by Bar Harbor and Acadia National Park, which were lovely. We also took a short tour of the Roosevelt home at Campobello National Park, which is actually on the edge of Canada. We drove through New Brunswick and took the ferry from St

John to Nova Scotia on the way to Halifax. We visited the scenic Peggy's Cove and the museum at Lunensburg near Halifax where we saw the sailing ship featured on the reverse of the Canadian dime. We also visited the very educational Alexander Graham Bell's Museum and drove the Cabot's Trail on Cape Breton Island. Then, we drove through Prince Edwards Island on the return trip to New Brunswick.

One of the highlights of this trip was to see the famous Bay of Fundy tides at Hopewell Rocks, New Brunswick. The tide drops about 40 feet baring large sections of land on which we were able to walk at low tide. At St. John, we saw the Reversing Falls featured by the tide moving both directions up the river and back over a short period of time. On the way home from Nova Scotia, we spent a couple days at Cape Cod, never having been there before. It was a longer trip from Boston to Provincetown, Cape Cod, than I has expected. But, we had a good time savoring the beaches and the resort atmosphere. We drove by the celebrity town of Hyannis Port and stopped to see the aquarium at the famous Woods Hole Research Center, before heading home.

# UNITED STATES AIR FORCE

Lackland Air Force Base

Scott Air Force Base

Service in Korea

Off Duty in Korea

## Lackland Air Force Base

*A* few weeks after graduation, in May 1953, Hazel and I trucked down to San Antonio, Texas to be activated into the Air Force at Lackland Air Force Base. The heat increased as we drove south in our 1950 Chevrolet Impala which, of course, had no air conditioning. By the time we reached San Antonio we thought we were burning up.

On the way, we passed by Waco, Texas and a couple weeks later we learned of the shocking damage that had been dealt to Waco by a tornado that stuck the town's business section.

In San Antonio, we found a small apartment at which we lived but we were there only one month. I think the temperature hit 100 degrees about every day we were there.

One event sticks in my mind during the short period of time that we were in San Antonio. I had a cousin, Neva Engelhoven, who was a close friend when we were growing up. She was the same age as I was and we attended Oskaloosa High School at the same time. Her mother was my Mother's sister, Engelene, and they lived in Oskaloosa so we got together quite often.

She went to Central College for a couple years and while there met and married a guy named Hershel Douglas. He was in the Naval Air Command and at the time we were in San Antonio, they were stationed at the naval airbase at Kingville, Texas. It is located within the King Ranch, about 125 miles from San Antonio, not far from Corpus Christi. The King Ranch is the largest ranch in the country and covers most of the county. It is famous for the Santa Gretudis cattle that it developed and still raises 50 years later. We decided to drive down and spend a weekend with Neva and Hershel. We had a fun time with them and their three kids.

Hershel was a very interesting guy and full of stories of his many escapades in the Navy. He was doing a lot of flying, particularly in the Far East, and had been behind enemy lines during the early part of the Korean War doing secret missions in China. One of the things we did together that weekend was to go rattlesnake hunting on the King Ranch. He only had a handgun, which did not worry me much because he apparently was a crack shot with it. I only worried when he gave me the gun. Fortunately, we only saw one snake and it was swimming across a river. In 1957, Hershel was reported missing while on a reconnaissance mission flying near China, and never heard from again.

Neva returned to Central College to complete her education. She met another man there whom she married in 1959. Her new husband, Rev. Vogelaar, was a Reformed Church missionary

United States Air Force

to Egypt and they spent most of their lives ministering there to the Arab Muslims and Christians. Neva had two more children. She was a religious person and taught in the same places as her husband, who was a university professor. The sad thing is that when they returned from Egypt to retire, she developed Alzheimer's disease and died in 1998 at age 67. We had seen Neva only once or twice since our weekend together in Texas.

## Scott Air Force Base

From Lackland, I was assigned to Scott Air Force Base, Illinois, to attend the 43-week Officer's Communications Course. It was located about 20 miles east of St. Louis. I attended classes at Scott six hours a day, from 6:00 a.m. until noon. We learned how to build tube radios, communicate with Morse code, and use other forms of communication that seem archaic now, but that was 50 years ago.

We rented a house off base on Mary Jane Street in Lebanon, Illinois located about five miles from the base. It was our first single-family dwelling and we were very happy with it. The big event of the year for us was the arrival of our first child, Stephen Wayne. He was born December 18, 1953, in a hospital at the neighboring town of Highland, Illinois, about 10 miles from home. The doctor was not in the Air Force but a pleasant local doctor. It cost us about $500, which seemed like a lot of money at the time but it pales compared with medical costs today. Of course, my monthly paycheck was only about $200.

Another thing I remember about living there was having my two lower wisdom teeth pulled at the base dentist. They had to be dug out since they were impacted against my other teeth. At least the Air force paid the bill so that made it less painful. But, we enjoyed living there and made several friends in the neighborhood. We also enjoyed occasionally visiting St. Louis. We particularly liked the zoo with their large apes and gorillas. It is one of the best zoos in the country.

Upon completion of the Communication's School in April or May 1954, I was assigned to go to Korea and serve as a Communications Officer. Hazel and our young son moved to Iowa for the year I was gone to Korea. They lived on the farm with my parents. That was a new experience for my wife, living with her in-laws and having been reared in town with a corner grocery store nearby. At least she had a car to drive but she was not too proficient with driving since she only learned to drive after we were married.

## Service in Korea

I was assigned to Fifth Air Force Headquarters at K-55, Oson, Korea, located about 30 miles south of Seoul. My job was to serve as a duty officer at a teletype relay center. It was one of four such positions, and when I arrived I was surprised to find that the other three duty officers were from my class back at Scott Air Force Base. The four of us manned the operations of the relay center 24 hours a day, seven days a week, with one of us on duty at all times. We rotated to a different shift every week. The fourth person among us was off duty for the week.

My trip to Korea was arduous but interesting. In those days there were no direct flights to Asia from the U.S. I flew on a C-124 from Hickum Field airbase in California; I flew backwards all the way to Japan since the seats all faced to the rear. We stopped in Honolulu to refuel, which gave me a chance to visit a college friend briefly who was stationed there near the airport. From there we flew to Wake Island again to refuel, and from there we were supposed to make it to Japan. However, we developed engine problems so we were diverted to Iwo Jima. There, we spent the night and resumed our flight to Tachacowa Air Base in Japan, not far from Tokyo, the next day.

That evening in Iwo Jima, a group of us were able to get some local airmen to take us up Mount Suribachi to see the place where the Marines had raised the famous flag when Iwo was liberated. They have the original monument of which the one in Washington DC is a replica. We were warned to stay on the path around the monument because the mountainside still contained live ammunition. At that time, 1954, it had been only about nine years since the end of World War II.

We stayed in Japan for a few days before flying on to Korea and we were able to do some local sightseeing prior to leaving. I flew to Korea in a C-46 airplane, a rather old plane even by standards of that day. That was an experience. The plane had bucket seats, meaning that we sat in rows on either side of the plane with our backs to the widows. The seats were really just metal ledges with indentations designed to accommodate troops wearing parachutes on which they sat facing the middle of the plane. I don't recall if we wore parachutes or not, probably not, although I had trained with them. The middle of the plane was piled high with our duffle bags and sundry supplies tied down. Fortunately, it was only 500-600 miles to Seoul.

When we arrived at Kimpo Airport at Seoul, on the

banks of the Han River, we had no difficulty recognizing that it was a recent war zone. It was May 1954 and the fighting in Korea had stopped with the signing of an armistice the previous October. Sand bags were piled high around the terminal and the tarmac where they parked their planes. Several F-86's were idling at the end of the runways ready for takeoff in case of attack. We were only about 30 miles south of the demilitarized zone (DMZ) separating North Korea from South Korea. Tensions were rather high. Rifles were stacked along the walls of the flight terminal ready for use. We also arrived in the middle of a celebration for the Secretary of Defense who was being greeted as we were disembarking from our plane. I have forgotten his name.

 Rather soon we were loaded into trucks and taken to K-55 located south of Seoul on a dusty gravel road. This base looked rather similar to the one at Seoul. Sand bags were piled high everywhere, including around the communications center where I worked. We had four F-86 jets standing at the end of one runway with engines running all the time I was in Korea. When they were up on training flights they occasionally broke the sound barrier, which was unmistakable when it happened. They were not supposed to do it over the base.

 We lived in the bachelor officers' quarters (BOQ) barracks consisting of tin Quonset huts. Our building had two rows of cots lined up inside, about six feet apart. We had a Korean Mama-son to sweep the floor, keep things in order, and keep the fire burning in our kerosene stove during the winter. Our bathroom was in the next building and actually served several barracks. The weather was rather similar to what I had been accustomed to in the Midwest. The officers all ate in a central cafeteria where the food was prepared and served mostly by Korean women. This cafeteria served perhaps 10 buildings of officers. The food was okay, except they never served ice cream, which I craved before going to Japan for rest and recuperation (R&R) after about six months.

  My stay in the BOQ was comfortable but rather uneventful. We did not have any security problems that I was aware of. Also living in our building was a civilian employee who worked with us on technology and was a colorful character. He was a competent worker keeping our teletype machines working, but the thing I remember most about him was that he was a heavy scotch drinker. First thing in the morning, he liked to gargle with his scotch to wake himself. Our captain also stayed in our building. He had a Rolex watch, with oyster perpetual date, and was very proud of it. I expect that is why I bought one myself, several years later in St. Thomas. One morning, one of the Second Lieutenants, a friend of mine, was found dead in his bed. His building was only a short distance across from ours. I never heard what caused his death, but it appeared to be from natural causes.

Our job was to oversee the receipt of messages by radio from Japan and to resend them to their final destinations using paper tape. We manually resent them to the various air bases located around South Korea, of which there were about a dozen. We had a continual flow of messages, and the paper tapes that we used were piled high by the end of each day; when they were burned. Our operations center employed 25-30 men. Close to the end of my tour I was promoted to First Lieutenant and for a short while was the operations officer in charge of the entire teletype operation. We reported to a major who commanded the Second Squadron, of which we were a part. He never gave us any problems. In fact, we didn't see him often; his office was about a half mile away.

## Off Duty in Korea

The four duty officers, of whom I was one, had a jeep assigned to them. We occasionally used it for excursions into the countryside when not on duty. We enjoyed touring the area, which included Suwon about 10 miles away. It is an ancient city with an old stonewall surrounding it.

Farmers in the area raised mostly rice and did it the old fashioned way, planting and harvesting by hand and carrying it away on "A" frames on their backs. Occasionally, however, we did see a water buffalo pulling a plow through the muddy water prior to planting. The people lived mostly in thatched huts crowded together. They were poor, but friendly and I visited them on various occasions. We took turns being the duty officer for the base, which did not happen often because it was a large base. One night in that capacity, in the wee hours of the morning, we went looking for GI's in the surrounding village who were not supposed to visit the local girls. We found one—it was an eye-opening experience.

There was a large post exchange (PX) located in Seoul that sold a greater variety of goods than our local PX so we occasionally went to Seoul for shopping and sightseeing. Any time we left the base, we were armed with our 45 caliber handguns.

We practiced occasionally, but found that it was difficult to hit anything more than a stone's throw away. The 45s also had a real kick to them so you needed both hands on them if you had any hope of hitting your target. We just hoped that they had a deterrent effect on anyone wanting to cause problems.

On a return trip from Seoul, one afternoon we were riding down the main road in a jeep full of officers and heard a large crack. We thought we had blown a tire so we pulled over to the side to investigate. The tires were fine, but then we saw a small hole in the canvass on either side of the rear seat about waist high—we got out of there as quickly as we could. Although we did not see anyone, it was obvious that a rifle had been fired at us.

Another harrowing experience occurred one day when four of us were out driving on the back roads toward the Yellow Sea that was perhaps 20 miles from our base. As we approached the ocean, coming over a small hill, we saw a barbed wire surrounding what appeared to be a small enclosed area with some targets sitting on the beach. We got out of the jeep studying the situation to see what we had found. About that time we heard a tremendous noise overhead and a fighter plane flew over us just above the low treetops with guns blazing, with another one right behind.

We hit the ground as quickly as we could, thankful to be alive. Obviously, by then we realized that this was a gunnery range for the fighter planes. We got out of there as quickly as we could but not before they had made a second pass above us. They did not seem to even see us.

My wife sent me many photographs she took of our son, Stephen. We had a base photo shop where I learned to develop my own pictures. I also spent a lot of time in the library; I think I read most of the books there during that year. I also signed up for a course on the history of Asia. The Air Force hired a professor from southern California to teach the course. It was very informative. The other activity at which I spent a lot of time was playing pool at the officer's club. At one point, I represented the base at a billiards' competition in Tago and came in second place.

I had an interested experience during a visit one time to Inchon, the site of McArthur's invasion that pushed the North Koreans back north after they had pushed the U.S. and South Korean Armies almost to Pusan. The U.N. had a delegation visiting there to monitor the armistice. I had one occasion to go there, but cannot now remember why. I had a very friendly conversation with a Russian I met there who was a part of the U.N.

delegation.

Fifth Air Force had a small plane that made a "milk run" visiting the various bases all over South Korea, mainly to deliver the mail. We could ride along occasionally if we wanted to see the sights. I once took the opportunity to visit a friend of mine from our Communication School at Scott Air Force Base who was stationed up near the DMZ, the dividing line with North Korea. Their facilities were rather spartan compared with ours; they lived in tents.

Once during the year I was in Korea I was sent on R&R to Japan, to Tokyo and a side trip to Nagoya. My brother, Dave, was in the Army stationed in Hokkaido, the northernmost providence in Japan, at the time so we arranged to meet in Tokyo for a few days and then we went to a military resort for another few days located about an hour by train north of Tokyo. We had a real fun time together seeing the sights of Tokyo and doing some shopping on the Ginza. We both put on civilian clothes because I was an officer and he was an enlisted man, which might have raised questions for those seeing us together. We stayed in hotels in the central section of the city that catered only to service men, but Dave and I stayed in different hotels.

Then, I went to Nagoya for two or three days. It was primarily to visit the factory where Naritake china is made. That factory was fascinating to see. I purchased a 12-place-setting of beautiful china that I had shipped home. It cost me less than $100 to buy and ship it home in a crate. We still have the china more than 50 years later and it has stood the test of time very well. I also took a bus excursion of the city of Nagoya. The guide was a cute little Japanese girl who spoke only Japanese. I could see the sights even if I did not know what I was seeing. It was a lovely city.

    Another interesting experience occurred after I had been in Korea several months. I had just come out of the Operations Center at about 6:00 a.m. one morning on the way to get breakfast after working the night shift. Looking up, I saw the strangest sight I had ever seen. There, I saw what I am still convinced, was a flying saucer. It was very clear to me. It was perhaps 1,000 feet high and standing very still, making no sound. It was just getting light, but the saucer had windows rimming the entire body that were brightly lit. The body of the ship was dark in color, perhaps 50 or 60 feet in diameter, and 10-15 feet tall, shaped just like a saucer. I stood there frozen and stared at it, hoping that some of my men who were going to breakfast with me would come out of the building, to verify what I was seeing. I did not want to go in to get them because I might miss something. Unfortunately, none of them came out until the saucer backed up and flew away noiselessly.

I told my captain what I had seen when I returned to the barracks that morning and asked him if I should report it. He said: *"you've been up all night and it was about daybreak so you probably imagined it."* He was right, that would probably be the reaction to anyone I told of it, so I did not report it officially. I just sat down and wrote a letter to my wife telling her all of the details but did not tell anyone other than the captain.

I returned home in May 1955 and was deactivated from the Air Force on schedule at the end of my two-year tour. I weighed out of the Air Force at about 185 pounds, a few more than I went in with but have remained close to that level since then. They also told me that my cholesterol at 200 was a little too high so I stopped eating butter and some other fatty foods which apparently helped because I have never had it tested that high since then.

# GRADUATE SCHOOL

Master's Degree

Doctor of Philosophy

Travels in California

## Master's Degree

After my career in the Air Force, I returned to Iowa State in May 1955 to look for a job after staying in Oskaloosa for a few weeks of leave. After a brief interview, I was offered a full-time position at the Iowa Agriculture Extension Service working as the assistant to Francis Kutish, a professor in the Agriculture Economics Department. The job paid $4,000 per year and I was expected to help Mr. Kutish develop price projections, write the weekly Iowa Farm Outlook Letter that was sent primarily to Iowa farmers, and give speeches to farm groups discussing the outlook for farm product prices (Hiemstra, 1955-57). Francis Kutish had a national reputation for doing agricultural price and farm production projections. He taught me the tricks of the trade and awakened in me a real interest in doing price projections. I continued doing price projections throughout my subsequent positions at USDA and Purdue University, often as a sideline.

I learned to write by writing sections in the Outlook Letter and on occasion writing the whole thing when Francis was out of town. I also had to give speeches to various farm groups when Francis was otherwise engaged. I still remember the panic of giving my first major address, given to the Iowa Sheep Growers Association in a large hotel auditorium in Des Moines.

I was also told that I could take courses on a part-time basis that would count toward a Master's Degree in agricultural economics, if I wanted to. I could get payments of something like $90 per month under the GI Bill of Rights to pay for my efforts. I did not need to pay tuition since I was a university employee. This sounded too good to pass up so I enrolled, even though I had no real interest in doing graduate studies at the time. But, my interest increased as I began to study.

We lived first in an apartment in downtown Ames in the top floor of a parsonage of a Lutheran minister. We often attended his church. I remember living there during the fall of the year, since I used to go squirrel hunting with my friend Wayne Fuller. My wife did not mind my hunting, but she did mind my dressing out the carcasses of the squirrels I shot by hanging them up from the door frame above our bathroom door. Later, we moved into the university's married student housing at 643 Pammel Court just north of the campus. It was not lavish accommodations. The units were made of tin, complete with tin roofs, that had been built for students returning to school after World War II but they had two bedrooms. We bought new furniture, including our first television (TV). The TV, of course, ran on tubes that burned out

*Graduate School*   65

rather frequently but I learned how to change them.

We were only about a block from the train tracks going through the university part of Ames, but we got used to the noise. While living there, our second child, Diane Sue, was born on April 4, 1956, while I was attending a class in economics. I had taken my wife to the Lafayette hospital during the wee hours of that morning, but did not expect Diane to arrive so soon.

I remember one morning that winter when the temperature was -30 F, the coldest day I ever remember in Iowa. Of course, my car would not start so I walked to work. It was bitterly cold so I walked through as many buildings as possible along the way. It was about one mile to my office across campus.

I earned my master's degree over a two-year period taking courses two at a time. At the master's level, I learned that studying economics is heavily dependent on the application of calculus and statistical analysis. My master's thesis was based upon the development of a multiple regression, a statistical model to project the number of pigs to be farrowed the following season based on the earlier prices of corn and other contributing factors. It was labeled *"Forecasting Quarterly Sow Farrowings."* Francis Kutish served as my thesis advisor.

I came close to ending my education and taking a job

offered to me doing poultry extension work at Virginia Tech in Blacksburg, Virginia. I was invited to Blacksburg for an interview but I was not impressed because the town was in the middle of nowhere. Even though it was considered to be a good job, I decided to study for a doctor of philosophy (Ph. D.) degree at the University of California at Berkeley, where I had already been accepted.

Actually, I had also applied for a couple price forecasting positions in the livestock industry, one working for a small meat packing plant in Kansas City and the other working for Morrell meat packing company in their headquarters in Chicago. Had either of those jobs materialized, I likely would not have gone on for a Ph.D. degree.

## Doctor of Philosophy

I had applied for a half-time assistantship at Berkeley to begin study in fall 1957 but was told in the spring that it had gone to someone else. I decided at that time to go anyway and try to live on the GI Bill. We were accepted to live in university housing at Berkeley, which would not cost too much ($46 per month). But, over the summer, I was told that the original recipient had declined their offer and they wanted to know if I still wanted it. I readily accepted because the $220 per month it provided more than doubled the money we would have had available and I would not need to pay tuition with the assistantship. I was paid full-time during the summers and during the entire third year that doubled the above income. These funds were provided by a grant from the Farm Foundation.

I was still able to get full-time student benefits under the GI Bill, which amounted to $160 per month the first school year. I was expected to perform half-time duties for one of the professors in response to my assistantship. Much of that work contributed indirectly toward my studies because I was helping a couple professors doing marketing research studies, particularly during the third year when I was writing my dissertation.

We moved to Berkeley in June 1957 by pulling a large

trailer behind our 1953 Chrysler containing all of our furniture. That was a harrowing trip; fortunately my car had a straight transmission that I could gear down while going over the mountains. I should not have overloaded the trailer like I did, but we got there. It was a real challenge going over Donner Pass on Route 40 in low gear, but we made it. A few months after arriving in Berkeley, I had a new motor put in my car. But, in those days a new motor was not prohibitively expensive.

We lived first in a house in East Oakland next to that of Ken and Mary Farrell, while awaiting entry into university housing in the fall. Ken was on the faculty at Berkeley at the time, working for the California Agricultural Extension Service. He had received his Ph.D. degree at Iowa State a year or two prior to our arrival at Berkeley, so we knew them well. They found us the house. I was impressed that it had a lemon tree in the back yard. Ken was Canadian and had his undergraduate degree from the Ontario Agricultural College at Guelph, Hazel's hometown[1]. Mary grew up in England.

Berkeley's married student housing development was located in Albany, California near San Francisco Bay and a

---

[1] Last summer, we attended Ken Farrell's 80th birthday. They now live in Walnut Creek, CA, not far from Berkeley.

horseracing track. It was only about two miles from the Berkeley campus. After moving there, I bought a bicycle and rode it to campus most of the three years that we lived there.

I studied under several competent professors at Berkeley. Agricultural econometricians in our department taught our statistics courses from the perspective of agriculture, so we did not need to go to the statistics department for statistics classes. These professors included George Kusnets who taught the basic courses in statistical analysis focusing on the fine points of multiple regression analysis and fitting simultaneous equations. I don't recall him ever using notes in his presentations of complicated statistical procedures. I was impressed that he was the brother of the Kusnets who had developed the national income accounts for the U.S. Bureau of Labor Statistics back in the 1930s.

Ivan Lee followed Kusnets with a course on maximum likelihood statistical procedures. Professor Jim Boles taught another statistical course focused on the theoretical basis of various tests to validate the assumptions upon which the basic statistical procedures rested.

Jim Boles also taught all of us graduate students that were interested to play bridge. He was an accomplished player and he encouraged us to bring bag lunches at noon during which we all played bridge in the lunchroom for precisely one hour each day.

George Mehron was Head of the Giannini Foundation of Agricultural Economics, as our department was named. Mr. Giannini, from Bank of America, had earlier made a major grant to our department. Mehron taught one of the marketing courses focused on analysis of marketing orders and agreements that were common among California's fruit and vegetable growers.

Professors Norman Collins, David Clarke, and Ray Bressler taught other marketing courses. Bressler was a leading marketing economist in the area of measuring production costs and economies of scale in food processing companies. Hearing him give an eloquent analytical presentation at Iowa State the previous year had inspired me to study at Berkeley.

Professor Andreas Papandreou, in the Economics Department, taught basic courses on economic principles. He was a Greek who returned to Greece a few years later and became a controversial prime minister. Papandreou became well known for his anti-American biases that I could never understand because I knew he was an accomplished economist, and I knew that he was married to a woman from Minnesota. I remembered him well for another reason too. He gave me the only grade less than an "A" that I received at Berkeley; he gave me a "B" because he did not like my term paper on the subject of welfare economics. I tried to defend the use of cardinal (absolute) utility as opposed to ordinal (relative) utility as a measurement of welfare economics. Papandreou was not impressed.

Professor Joe Bain was another outstanding professor at Berkeley who was a leader in analyzing the economics of antitrust law. He was also in the Economics Department, and I took both of his two graduate courses because my dissertation was focused on an analysis of industry structure.

My specialization within agricultural economics was in marketing with a special interest in the competitive nature of industry structure. My dissertation was an analysis of the structure of the retail food business in California. The growing consolidation of the retail food industry had been an ongoing national policy concern since the mid-1930s. I tried to address these concerns and incorporate some of the antitrust principles I had learned from Professor Bain. My dissertation was entitled, *"An Analysis of Forces Affecting the Procurement of Merchandise by Retail Grocery Firms."*

Professor Barton DeLoach chaired my dissertation committee and the other members included Professors Norman Collins and Lee Preston. I had the benefit of considerable information obtained personally from Safeway Corporation. Their corporate headquarters was located next door in Oakland California and their chief economist, Paul Baumgart, was a good friend of Barton DeLoach and very interested in my study. He was quite helpful to me. They later duplicated my dissertation for their own use.

DeLoach moved from Berkeley to the Los Angeles campus of the University of California (UCLA) during the summer of 1959, about the time I passed by written "prelim" exams and started working full-time on my dissertation. But, he still continued as Chairman of my committee. I traveled to UCLA for a couple days about every month to consult with him, because we remained living at Berkeley. I traveled on Southwest Airlines, one of the first discount airlines with reasonable prices. I used to stay at a motel in Westwood, next to the UCLA campus.

Word processors as we know them today were not available in 1960. I composed my dissertation on an old Underwood typewriter. It took me about 12 months to finish my dissertation from the time of my written exams, but of course I had begun working on it perhaps a year earlier. The oral exam on my dissertation was held in June 1960, which was the final step in receiving the degree. I later shortened and revised my dissertation and it was published by the California Agricultural Experiment Station, University of California, as a station bulletin: *Growth Patterns in the Retail Grocery Business* (Hiemstra and Deloach, 1962). It was my first major publication.

My officemate during the first two years was Dick Coutche, from Arizona. We became good friends. He was a good golfer, and helped me with my game whenever we could find time. We usually played on the mountain slopes above the campus at a public course. Dick found the Ph.D. program requirement too tough and dropped out after two years and returned to Arizona to become a stockbroker. I visited him once a few years later and he seemed to be doing well. The third year I had an officemate from India named Agarwal (forgot his first name). The main thing I remember about Agarwal was that he wanted me to teach him how to drive a car. I worked with him for months and finally he got his driver's license. That afternoon, driving alone for the first time, he got into a car accident.

## Travels in California

We loved living in California, particularly Northern California, and thought we would move back there sometime in the future but we never did. Fortunately, we did do a fair amount of traveling about the state in our spare time. San Francisco is a fascinating place to visit. The hills are a challenge just driving up and down their steep slopes, which are better suited for the cable cars.

China Town is a unique place to visit with all of the Asian culture and unusual products for sale. We visited it often, along with the nearby Fisherman's Warf. We liked to drive down Lombard Street, the *"crookedest street in the world,"* to the light house looking out on San Francisco Bay toward Alcatraz. We also loved to visit Yosemite National Park with its majestic views and its huge Sequoia trees.

Marin County was another beautiful place to visit. Muir Woods has a stand of beautiful Sequoia trees in Mount Tamelpais State Park. They are not as grand as those at Yosemite but still impressive. We found a lovely beach just north of the Golden Gate Bridge that we visited often. It was reachable only by driving through a missile installation that guarded the city and then walking down a steeply inclined path on the ocean side of the Golden Gate Bridge to reach the very small but lovely beaches. Needless to say, it was quite private. I doubt we would be allowed there these days because of security concerns. It is awesome to view the Golden Gate Bridge up from ground level near the north piers, not far from Sausalito. We also enjoyed visiting Golden Gate Park and the zoo on the western edge of the city.

Another place we enjoyed visiting was Mount Diablo State Park, a few miles east of Walnut Creek. It had a beautiful view of the entire area from the peak. One time we were driving up Mount Diablo and stopped for a picnic with the kids. There was a pine tree nearby that had some lovely pine cones on it that were larger than any we had ever seen. I climbed up a few limbs and picked several of those pinecones, some of which we still have today, 50 years later. We probably broke some law in the process but we were not aware of it at the time. Another beautiful place in Northern California that we enjoyed visiting was the wine country at Napa Valley.

The first school year we lived in Berkeley, we took the train to Iowa and back to visit my parents between semesters in late January 1958. That train ride was quite scenic in going through the Rocky Mountains, but it was a long overnight ride with the kids. That summer we drove to Pullman Washington in August to attend meetings of the Western Farm Economics Association to present a paper. That was a lovely drive, passing Mount Shasta in Northern California as well as Crater Lake and Klamath Falls across the border in Oregon. Crater Lake is extremely deep and has the bluest water imaginable. We also drove close enough to Mount St. Helens to see it well, before heading east to Pullman.

Another time, on a trip from California, we stopped by Lake Tahoe when the winter Olympics were soon to be held nearby in the Sierra Nevada Mountains. We watched the skiers practicing their jumps off a high mountain slope and were much impressed. Another time, I helped a friend of mine from our church in Berkeley[1] who was building a house on the shore of Lake Tahoe. The house got built but unfortunately he died a couple years later. He was the Berkeley High School basketball coach.

In July 1959 we drove to Utah to attend the annual meetings of the American Farm Economic Association meetings at Logan, and then drove on to Oskaloosa for a vacation before returning to California. We always stopped to see various attractions on our cross-country trips. Driving East from Salt Lake City, for example, we stopped at a dinosaur museum that was

---
1 First Presbyterian Church, Berkeley, California

fabulous. We ran into some good friends of ours there, Martha and Lee Schrader. Lee was a fellow graduate student of mine at Berkeley. They eventually took a job in the Agricultural Econ Department at Purdue University, so we saw a lot of them later when we moved to West Lafayette.

In December 1959, we took a family vacation trip to Los Angeles. We visited Disneyland and Marineland and planned to stay over January 1 to see the Rose Bowl Parade. But, it turned cold and we did not have enough warm clothes for the kids so we headed back a day early, planning instead to stop and visit the Hearst Castle on the scenic drive back home on U.S. 101. However, after arriving there we discovered that the Castle closed one day per year, on New Year's Day. We tried once more a couple decades later to get into the Castle, but it was too crowded that day so we never did get to see it.

But, we did see the 17-Mile Drive and the Pebble Beach Golf Course at Monterey on that New Years' Day. My friend Paul Baumgart from Safeway had a house nearby to which he retired several years later. We visited him there one time but never found time to accept his invitation to play golf at his course. We actually visited Monterey and Pebble Beach several times while we lived in California. I attended a conference there one time and played golf at one their courses, but not Pebble Beach.

One of the primary reasons we enjoyed our time in Berkeley so much was due to our membership in the First Presbyterian Church of Berkeley all of the time we were in California. The pastor at the time, Dr. Robert Boyd Munger[2], was an outstanding preacher and the people of the church made us feel very much at home. We made many friends in the church, in part, because of the gregarious leadership of his assistant pastor, Don Mumau. In June 1958, our church was active in supporting the Billy Graham crusade held at the Cow Palace in San Francisco. I served as one of the ushers at the crusade and was quite impressed with the Billy Graham team.

On our final trip back from Berkeley to Washington DC in September 1960 we drove through Death Valley. We were a little early in the season for driving through Death Valley and it was very hot, 107 degrees. We had a flat tire not far from where we planned to camp for the night at Furnace Creek. It was very hot for tent camping and a little spooky, since we were about the only people there and somewhat concerned about snakes. We gave up trying to sleep about 4 a.m. and headed out. There was no auto service at Furnace Creek to fix our tire. We had to drive

---

2 Dr. Munger later joined the faculty at Fuller Theological Seminary in Pasadena, California. He is famous for a sermon that was published: *My Heart, Christ's Home* (2001).

about 100 miles before we could get our tire repaired so it was good that we had started early before it got too hot.

From there we drove through Las Vegas, stopping to go on an excursion down into Hoover Dam. That is an amazing facility, considering that it was built during the 1930s. It is now closed from visitors due to security concerns. We then drove to the North Rim of the Grand Canyon, Zion National Park and Bryce Canyon in Utah, which are among the most beautiful sights in the country. From there we drove through Iowa to visit relatives and on to the Washington DC area. That was a fabulous trip.

# ECONOMIC RESEARCH SERVICE, USDA

Marketing Economics Division

Economic and Statistical Analysis Division

Interesting Travel

Professor DeLoach, my major professor at Berkeley, had been an employee of the Economic Research Service (ERS) in the U.S. Department of Agriculture (USDA), Washington DC, prior to his going to the University of California. He encouraged me to take a job in his former organization when I completed my degree. He had taken me to Washington one time and introduced me to many of his former colleagues at ERS and I was impressed with their research efforts and their publications. I applied for a position with ERS and they offered me a job during June 1960. I worked at ERS till I joined the Food Nutrition Service (FNS) in December 1969.

ERS could only give me a GS-11 level salary at that time, which was below the going market at universities for Ph.D.s in my field at the time. I had earlier interviewed with the Agricultural Economics Department at Purdue University and they had offered me a job for at least $1,000 more money. But, I was not interested in teaching at the time. I preferred a research position at USDA so I agreed to the ERS salary if they would pay my moving expenses to Washington DC.

USDA did not normally pay such expenses for new employees at that time. But, they agreed to hire me to work for about three months with a small group of ERS employees working at the Post Office in Berkeley. That put me on salary sooner and, as an USDA employee, ERS was able to pay my moving expenses to Washington. Because I had a wife and two children, plus a lot of furniture, this was an important consideration. Of course, being put immediately on the payroll was also a benefit. I was promoted to GS-12 soon after being with USDA the minimum of 12 months in grade.

We moved to Alexandria, Virginia in September. My new boss, Paul Nelson, had found us a townhouse in Fairlington, the same area in which he lived. By coincidence I worked just a few blocks from there several years later when I was working for FNS. We lived at 3704 King Street for one year. During this time, we were members of Fairlington Presbytrian Church and Karen Lee, who was born on July 7, 1961, was baptized there by my brother, Rev. John E. Hiemstra.

A year later, we bought a house in Lanham, Maryland, at 6808 Trexler Road, off of Good Luck Road. We joined Grace Presbyterian Church, a small church in Lanham, and I was elected elder. I later served as their church treasurer for a couple years. Our house was new, in fact, it had been a model home for the new subdivision just being built at the time. In a couple years, we had enough people in the neighborhood to organize a community swimming pool. I served as president of that pool the year it was opened. Our son, John David, was born on April 9, 1963 while we lived there.

After a few years, Grace's pastor left and we joined Riverdale Presbyterian Church which had a pastor that we liked. At Riverdale, I again served as an elder and we made some long-lasting friendships, including the Dunns, the Estells, the Regans, the Jenkins, and the Iffts. Ted Ifft later invited me to join his golf group which played at the University of Maryland golf Course.

I worked at the USDA's South Building at the corner of Independence Avenue and 14th Street, near the Mall and the Washington Monument. Over our lunch hour, we often got our exercise by walking up the steps of the Monument (555 feet), which offers a great view on top.[1]

We also used to visit other nearby monuments on the mall over lunchtime, like Freer Art Gallery and the National Museum of American History. The exhibits in both were interesting and the history building also had a great cafeteria.

I commuted to Washington by bus initially and later by carpool. Parking spaces within the building's courtyards were re-

---

[1] In recent years the Monument's steps have been closed because too many walkers suffered heart attacks and could not be easily rescued.

served for car pools with four or more members so most people tried to organize such pools. At that time, there was no metro subway system in Washington and the commuter traffic was very heavy.

### Marketing Economics Division

*M*y first job at USDA was a research position with ERS working for Paul Nelson, Head of the Market Structure and Analysis Section. This section was in Bob Olsen's Branch and Kenneth Ogren's Division, the Marketing Economics Division. Eisenhower was still President when I arrived in Washington.

I was soon writing articles that appeared in the Marketing and Transportation Situation (MTS) published under the auspices of our division. For example, in February 1962 I co-authored with Forrest Scott a long article *"The Food Marketing Industry Recent Changes and Prospects,"* (Scott and Hiemstra, 1962). It was published as a special article in MTS and focused on changes in numbers and sales of retail, wholesale, and manufacturing food establishments and companies over the period 1947 to 1958 based largely on analysis of U.S. Census data for 1958, 1954, and 1947. In August 1962, I authored a related article called *"Concentration and ownership in food manufacturing industries,"* (Hiemstra, 1962a). It used the census data to measure changes in concentration of business in the food industries by the larges 4 or 8 companies.

Later, I began to do more in-depth research on the general subject of profitability of food companies and how their profits should be measured and interpreted. This study led to a study of depreciation and how its measurement affects profits. It led to journal articles, "*Depreciation: A Rising cost of Processing Food Products,*" published in the *American Journal of Farm Economics* (AJFE) in August 1962, (Hiemstra, 1962b); and, "*Profits as a Measure of Profitability,*" published in the same journal a year later (Hiemstra, 1963a). It also led to a major bulletin published by ERS, *Rising Depreciation of Assets in Agricultural Marketing Firms, Some Causes and Implications,* (Hiemstra, 1963b).

From there, I focused on the importance of lease financing, particularly by food retailers that commonly leased their stores, and how leasing affects business risk and the measurement of profits by keeping assets used by the industry off of their balance sheets. This work led to publication of an article, "*Lease-Financing and Returns to Capital of Food Marketing Firms,*" published in *Agricultural Economics Research*, an in-house academic journal published by ERS (Hiemstra, 1962c). In more recent years, this subject became more familiar and more convoluted in the infamous Enron bankruptcy case.

I also submitted an article to the AJFE in response to a request for articles competing for cash awards. I won $250 for honorary mention at a time when that was a fair amount of money. It addressed the subject of the usefulness of using industry concentration ratios as a measure of competition, a controversial subject in those days. It cited a landmark court ruling in antitrust policy where such ratios were used successfully in a case called *United States v Philadelphia National Bank et al*. The article, "Concentration and Competition in the Food Industries," was published in the AJFE, (Hiemstra, 1966).

Unrelated to this work, but following up on my earlier work at Iowa State working as a livestock specialist, I was asked to join the Livestock and Meat Section of our Division part time in doing a rush study. ERS was mandated by the Congress to measure the importance of marketing lamb using federal grades. As a part of the study, we interviewed important participants in the industry, and I was asked to interview the major lamb producers and packers in California during the peak winter season. I flew out of Washington to California the day that a major snowstorm hit the city, which was also the day that John F. Kennedy was inaugurated as President. I missed the inauguration[1]. I may have been on the last plane out of Washington that day.

That was a pleasant and informative trip. I first talked to some meat packers as well as a sample of retailers in Los Ange-

---

1 Inauguration Day is a holiday for federal employees.

les[2]. I ended up interviewing the movers and shakers of the lamb industry at a critical time of the year at Brawley in the Imperial Valley of California. It is near the Mexican border in the middle of the state. This area has lush, green pastures of alfalfa where sheep and lambs nearly ready for slaughter feed during the coldest part of winter. It was a lovely place to visit at that time of year.

I helped author the final report with three other economists. It was a major ERS publication: *Economic Effects of US Grades for Lamb* (Fienup, Motes, Hiemstra and Laubis, 1963). An earlier version of the study was submitted to the Congress and published by them as a Committee Print of the House Committee on Agriculture in March 1962[3].

---

2 Even in the Watts area of Los Angeles riots later occurred.
3 *Effects of Federal Lamb and Mutton Grades on Producer and Consumer Prices* (Fienup, Motes, Hiemstra, and Laubis, 1962).

## Economic and Statistical Analysis Division

After two years in the Marketing Economics Division, I was offered the position as Head of the Food Consumption Section of the Economic and Statistical Analysis Division (ESAD) of ERS, working under Branch Chief Rex Daly. I was given a GS-13 level position as Acting Head immediately with promise of a GS-14 in 12 months as the official Head of the Section. ESAD did the price and output forecasting or "outlook" work for ERS. My Section had a staff of 10-12 people and was responsible for writing the National Food Situation (NFS) each quarter, under the overall watchful eye of the Outlook and Situation Board (ERS, 1963-69).

The NFS was responsible for publishing forecasts for retail food prices and estimates of per capita food consumption for USDA. It also published as special articles studies of demand for food and agricultural products. I ultimately was responsible for publishing 26 issues of the NFS (ERS, 1960 through 1969).

These reports were not authored publications because the Board took full responsibility for the contents. But, when we published special articles related to a special food price or food demand analysis, they were authored, even though they too had to pass approval of the Outlook Board. I published 16 such articles between 1963 to 1968. Five of them had joint authors.

The eminent Fred Waugh of food demand fame (Waugh, 1964) had been the Director of ESAD but retired soon after I arrived on the scene. Jim Cavin was our division director most of the time I was there, and Nathan Kofsky was the administrator of ERS. It was an exciting place to work because Kofsky was very supportive of our outlook and forecasting work. Rex Daly was also a very competent statistical analyst. In a sister Section of our Branch, he had a qualified staff of econometricians developing long-range projections under Alvin Egbert. These included Dawson Ahalt, who was a rising star at the time.

The NFS was one of a family of such situation reports, all but two of which were published by ESAD. They included the Livestock and Meat Situation, the Dairy Situation, the Poultry Situation, the Grain and Feed Situation, the Fats and Oils Situation, and the Farm Income Situation. I already mentioned that The Marketing and Transportation Situation was a member of this family but was prepared by the Marketing Economics Division rather than ESAD. The Foreign Trade Division also published a report called the Western Hemisphere Agricultural Situation.

Most of these situation reports have since been discontinued. In an attempt to be efficient after suffering many budget cuts over the years, USDA first collapsed their primary statistical outlet into a single monthly publication called *Agricultural Outlook* (ERS, 1975-2002). A decade after I left, The NFS was supplanted also in part by a new report, *National Food Review,* in 1978 and renamed the *Food Review* in 2002 (ERS, 1978-2004) but these reports were more marketing oriented than was NFS. In February 2003 both the *Food Review* and the *Agricultural Outlook* were replaced by a new report called *Amber Waves* (Economic Research Service, 2003-2004) which carries little of the outlook and situation material for which ERS had been famous.

*Amber Waves* is published 5 times per year and covers the broad scope of all ERS rural activities. ERS has lost a lot of agricultural economists over the years due to budget cuts and no longer devotes the resources to the subject that it once did. Much of the basic food and agricultural data previously published in *Agricultural Outlook* are now available on the internet.

When I was there, the situation reports were each written by their specified sections but they all had to be approved by the Outlook and Situation Board before they could be released. The 8-10 members of the Board would go over each report line-by-line and question any statement that was unclear or not in keeping with Board policy or in conflict with any other Situation report. These reviews often lasted three or four hours for each report. Getting the NFS approved each quarter was a challenge and taught me to write clearly, precisely, and grammatically correct.

Each year, ERS hosted the *Agricultural Outlook Conference*[1] focused primarily toward providing information to the outlook specialists in the Agricultural Experiment Stations located in the various states, at least in the early years. Every year from 1963 to 1969, I made a presentation to that Conference entitled, *"Outlook for Food Consumption, Prices, and Expenditures,"* and prepared a set of charts supporting the outlook, published in *Handbook of Agricultural Charts* (1963-67).

My presentations were published each year a few months after the Outlook Conference in the *Family Economics Review* by the Agricultural Research Service (ARS), (Hiemstra, 1963-67). In addition, for several years I would publish an article in the *Western Hemisphere Agricultural Situation*, summarizing the outlook for food in the U.S. (1964-66).

The people that published the *Family Economics Review* worked very closely with us in the Food Consumption Section, particularly Robert Rizek, Division Director, Betty Peterkin, and Berta Friend. Berta took our per capita food consumption data

[1] It is now called the Agricultural Outlook Forum.

and converted the amount of food consumed to the levels of individual nutrients that they represented, based upon detailed nutritional data in *Composition of Foods* (ARS, 1963 and following).

This report was commonly known as *Handbook No. 8* published by a sister agency of theirs in ARS, Consumer and Food Economics Research Division. Betty Peterkin had for years been computing the *"Thrifty Food Plan,"* which was published in the *Family Economics Review* and upon which the benefit levels of the FSP were later based (more on this in next chapter), even though it had been calculated many years earlier for nutrition education purposes.

Rizek's Division also conducted the *Household Food Consumption Survey* (HFCS) about once every decade, the last being in 1965. That survey was a massive effort that involved very detailed surveys of a national probability sample of individual households. Results of these surveys were used importantly for calculations of the various food plans, of which the *Thrifty Food Plan* was at the lowest income level.

These food plans were used by ARS specifically for their nutrition education efforts with various income levels. We in the Food Consumption Section also used the household consumption data from the HFCS surveys as food weights in computing the Food Consumption Index that was published quarterly in the NFS (Economic Research Service, 1963). Bob Rizek was a good professional friend of mine but he unfortunately died about the time I left ERS in 1969.

At that time, the Outlook Conference was held in November of the previous year under review; it is still being held to this day but the schedule was changed to delay the conference until spring of the current year tinder review. I was also a regular consultant to the public press on the subject of food price outlook, routinely getting phone calls from *Business Week*, *Forbes*, the *Wall Street Journal,* and other commentaries on the outlook for food prices. One year, *Value Line Investment Service* did me the honor of duplicating verbatim the summary sections from my NFS in one of their industry reviews of the food industry, but I never did talk to them. USDA reports, of course, are not copyrighted so it was no problem.

Each year, the Food Consumption Section updated and published a historical set of tables going back to 1909, giving per capita food consumption data in detail for each individual food product. It also included related data such as retail food prices by individual products published (detail was not published) by the Bureau of Labor Statistics, and food expenditures as published by the Department of Commerce. In addition, nutrients contained in the food estimated to be consumed were calculated for us by Berta Friend, ARS.

Of course, I had a lot of help in preparing my presentations at the Outlook Conference as well as the historic set of tables from my competent staff spearheaded by Helen Eklund who knew the numbers forward and backward. I also had a very capable secretary in those years, Jean (Hannold) Osterling, who could set up and type tables about as fast as most secretaries could type straight text. This was before the time of word processors.

Historically, the section would occasionally also publish a detailed report outlining the methodology used in calculating per capita food consumption data. When I became head of the section, such a detailed report had not been published for a decade, the last by Marguerite Burk (my predecessor) in 1952. We decided it was time for a major update because many changes had been made in the interim. As a result, we published a new and improved version, *U.S. Food Consumption, Sources of Data and Trends, 1909-63* (ERS, 1965). This report containing sources of data and procedures has not, to my knowledge, been subsequently updated.

Measuring food consumption was a detailed process involving the use of much unpublished data and certain estimates made by the Food Consumption Section and other outlook specialists in ESAD. Technically, the data were estimates of food disappearance or food used or not accounted for in the marketing system, rather than food actually known to have been eaten. We started with food commodities as computed at the farm level and adjusted it for:

1. Nonfood uses for feed and seed,

2. Imports, exports and government purchases for the military,

3. Retail equivalents using weight conversion factors allowing for losses in processing and marketing in order to make estimates of consumption at the retail level to match available retail food prices, and finally

4. Divided by total population, as of July 1, to compute per capita consumption.

We continued to update and publish these tables for three more years. Then, we developed a new primary report focused on analysis of the data rather than its sources and methodology. This report added a section measuring demand for food including some basic charts and statistical demand equations. The primary consumption and price data were updated but the table formats were modified and new information was provided, such as quarterly per capita consumption of livestock products, and retail price seasonality indexes. This report was entitled *Food Consumption, Prices, and Expenditures* (Hiemstra, 1968). This report's tables were subsequently updated almost every year through 1995, long after I had left ERS.

Each year since 1912, USDA has published and continues to publish a yearbook of agriculture, which is focused on a special topic. In both 1959 and 1969, it was focused on food and nutrition. I prepared an article for the 1969 Yearbook, *"Telescoping 20 years of Change in the Food We Eat,"* (Hiemstra, 1969). It highlighted some of the longer-term trends in food consumption. I collected these yearbooks, beginning with 1912 and still have most of them through about 1980.

In July, 1969, Al Egbert and I had published a study, *"Shifting Direct Government Payments from Agriculture to Poor People: Impacts on Food Consumption and Farm Income."* (Egbert and Hiemstra, 1969). It was based on data derived from a multi-year study by Al Egbert, Rex Daly, and others in our Branch to assess the impacts of government payments on agriculture. It was estimated that to raise the level of food consumption of all people with incomes below $3,000 to that of consumption of all people with incomes above $3,000 would cost $20 billion in income supplements. That was a lot of money in 1969.

We concluded that improving food programs like the Food Stamp Program (FSP) would be a more efficient way of raising nutritional levels than providing cash supplements. This study was followed by an article I published in the NFS called *"Food: A Special Issue in Welfare Programs"* (Hiemstra, 1970). The article was published shortly after I left ERS and joined FNS.

My article noted that the latest data at the time showed there was a lot of room for improvement in nutrition for low income people. Based on data from the USDA's *1965 Household Food Consumption Survey*, 36 percent of the households with annual incomes below $3,000 (roughly the poverty level at that time) had diets that failed to meet two-thirds of the nutrient levels recommended by the Recommend Dietary Allowances (RDA's) for all seven major nutrients studied. RDA levels are specified by the National Research Council of the National Academy of Science. Of course, income alone does not insure good nutrition. Nine percent of households with incomes above $10,000 also failed to meet the RDA test.

## *Interesting Travel*

I had some other interesting assignments while working for ERS, basically during the decade of the 1960s when I was employed as a professional economist. For example, I was invited to Puerto Rico for a month, September 5 through October 4, 1973, to help their Ministry of Agriculture calculate food consumption estimates for Puerto Rico. They wanted to parallel the U.S. data. We got the job done although they did not have all of the comparable statistical data available that we in the U.S. did, so some short cuts had to be made. The Ministry of Agriculture continued to publish the results years later; the last report I received was *Consumo De Alimentos En Pureto Rico*, 1950/51-1973/74, based on the methodology I developed with them. I had to brush up on my Spanish in the process; I had passed the Spanish reading requirement for my Ph.D. degree[1]. Fortunately, some of their people could speak English. When we communicated in writing it was usually in Spanish, but when speaking we resorted to English.

I took the family with me to San Juan, except for our son Stephen who was in college at the time. We lived in the Pierre Hotel in the Condado (tourist) region of the city. We took a couple trips to their rain forest named El Yongue National Park, and

1 I also studied German.

a beautiful beach nearby on the northeast coast of the island. El Yongue was on a mountain top, and we were fascinated by the tropical vegetation, including beautiful wild orchids living on many of the trees that subsisted entirely on the nearly daily rains. We also visited Mayaguez on the west coast of Puerto Rico where an agricultural branch of the University of Puerto Rico is located. I was there to visit the dean of the School of Agriculture. He was the brother of the person I worked for in San Juan. Mayaguez was also renowned for the several large tuna fish processing plants operating there at the time.

On the way across the island, we visited some mountainous s areas where they grow coffee beans and avocadoes. We also visited some pineapple and sugarcane plantations, although Puerto Rico's sugarcane production had been cut back severely, even by then, due to competition for available land and the rising costs of labor. We had an interesting time and met some helpful people. I returned to Puerto Rico many times later when I was working for FNS. Our son Stephen also went to Puerto Rico later to do an economic development study at the University of Puerto Rico near San Juan and wrote his master's thesis on the results.

About two weeks after returning from Puerto Rico, in mid-October, I attended the annual meeting of SM-34, a group of agricultural economists concerned with demand for food, meeting that year in Memphis, Tennessee. It was a Southern Regional project supported by ERS, and I was the ERS representative on the project as long as I was in ERS. The group was organized and managed by the Department of Agricultural Economics of the University of Georgia, located at their agricultural research facility near Atlanta. For the first several years, we met in Atlanta.

I continued to be a member of this group throughout the years I was in FNS, and until I retired from Purdue University in 1998. By then, it had expanded beyond the Southern Region to be nationwide in scope; it was then called S-216. We met at different places around the country, including twice in San Diego and once at the Coeur d'Aene Resort in Idaho, my last meeting. I was President of the group for two years and organized the annual meeting held in Las Vegas in 1995 at the Las Vegas Hilton Hotel. Analysis of demand for food was a continuing personal interest of mine throughout my career.

In February 1969, I was invited to present a paper on U.S. food consumption in Paris at the Centre National Des Exposition Et Concours Agricoles (CENECA) International Symposium (Hiemstra, 1969). That was a fine experience. The conference featured simultaneous translations of the presentations, just like the United Nations. I gave a talk focused on consumption of processed food in the United States. I represented the United States at the conference and was even honored with a reception hosted by the American Embassy in Paris. I bought myself a silk tie at the Embassy which became one of my favorites for years.

I enjoyed touring Paris, but quickly found that the best way to get around the city was by subway where I did not need to speak French to anyone. I tried taking a cab to the conference on the first day, but the taxicab got lost because the driver did not understand my English and I knew no French. I saw a subway stop, and I had a map and the address of the conference center, so I left the taxi and went on my own.

Thereafter, I either walked or took the subway; it was very easy to use without talking to anyone. An exception was in visiting Versailles, to which I took a bus because it is well out of the city.

Versailles was where the Peace Treaty of Paris was signed following World War I, where Marie Antoinette lived, and where the French Revolution had its origin. This building has several long halls lined with beautiful paintings and mirrors. The grounds too were breathtaking with endless gardens and lovely vistas. I visited many of the other major attractions in the city like the Eiffel Tower, Champs-Elysees, Notre-Dame, Arc de Triomphe, Napoleon's tomb, and the Louvre using my guidebook, *Europe on Five Dollars a Day* (2007). I stayed in an old hotel not far from the Opera House and other attractions. I came home with sore feet from the new shoes I was wearing.

At the conference, I met an earlier acquaintance from Berkeley who was a visiting professor from the Netherlands. He invited me to visit him at his University in Wageningen for a couple days before leaving Europe and I took him up on the invitation. I flew to Amsterdam and toured the city for a couple days, seeing the endless canals and windmills, the Van Gogh Museum, and the Rijks museum containing many Rembrandt paintings, of which I bought two or three small prints that would fit in my suitcase. I also visited the home of Anne Frank, the Jewish girl famous for her World War II diary. Then, I took a train to where the agricultural school was located.

Being a Dutchman by heritage, I enjoyed seeing some of the country of my ancestors. I was impressed that many people I encountered in Amsterdam spoke English. This is in contrast to Paris where they just stared at you. The Dutch went out of their way to help us Americans.

I was an active member of the American Agricultural

Economic Association (AAEA), which succeeded the AFEA, throughout my professional career. I joined when I moved to USDA in 1960 and continued my membership till after retiring in 1998. I published various articles in their journal particularly while I was in ERS, but continued to do so occasionally when I was at FNS and later at Purdue University. I attended their annual meetings almost every year for probably 20 years. The last year I was in ERS I attended the annual meetings held in Lexington, Kentucky in August.

I also occasionally attended the annual meetings of the American Economic Association (AEA) that were usually held between Christmas and New Year's Day as a component of the Allied Social Science Associations (ASSA). For example, I attended that meeting in New York City in December 1969. AAEA also held a second meeting each year ("winter" meetings) in conjunction with ASSA.

But, the main reason I attended AEA meetings was the fact that the Society of Government Economists (SGE) sponsored meetings each year at ASSA, and I was an active member of SGE. In that capacity, I often organized sessions and presented papers at the ASSE annual meetings. I was President of SGE for one year, about 1979 or 1980. It was an interesting group that allowed me to meet economists throughout Washington. I was an active member of SGE for perhaps 10 years, until 1983 when I retired from USDA and moved to West Lafayette, Indiana which is the home of Purdue University.

# FOOD NUTRITION SERVICE, USDA

New Assignment

Food Stamp Program

Child Nutrition Programs

Child Care Food Service

Women, Infants, and Children Program

Personal Travel

New Administration

## New Assignment

In December 1969, when I was 38 years old, I accepted a new position as Assistant to the Administrator of the Food and Nutrition Service. Howard Hjort, the chief economist of USDA at the time, had recommended me for the position. I had worked with Howard a lot and he knew of my interest in food demand analysis. I was put in charge of economic analysis and program evaluation of all of the domestic food assistance programs[1] operated by FNS. These programs included the Food Stamp Program (FSP), the School Lunch and Breakfast programs, the Child Care Programs, and a few lingering direct food distribution programs. Prior to that time, the food programs had been located in the Agriculture Marketing Service (AMS) because they were viewed importantly as efforts aimed at expanding the demand for agricultural products. The Woman, Infants, and Children Program (WIC) program was developed while I was at FNS.

FNS had been established to consolidate, expand, and re-target USDA's efforts at improving nutrition and reducing hunger and malnutrition of the recipients rather than just focus on marketing farm products. On May 6, 1969, a republican Presi-

---

1 A summary of these programs appears online at: http://www.fns.usda.gov/fdd/fdd-history-and-background.

dent, Richard Nixon, declared in a report to the Congress *"That hunger and malnutrition should persist in a land such as ours is embarrassing and intolerable."* He declared that *"the moment is at hand to put an end to hunger in America itself for all time."* He also directed that a White House Conference on Food, Nutrition and Health be held in the near future to address these issues.

The White House Conference was held in Washington DC in December 1969, and I attended along with the FNS Administrator, Edward J. Hekman, as one of my first assignments. At the Conference, and for the next several years after the Conference, there was a concerted effort to expand the food programs and make them more efficient (Hiemstra, 1978). But, there was a continual debate over food and income policies. Nutritionists and USDA wanted to give priority to food programs in supporting low-income people, in keeping with the mandates of FSP, whereas consumer advocates would have preferred that recipients receive unrestricted cash benefits to spend as they choose (Hiemstra, 1983). Subsequently, the poor people's march on Washington stressed this preference; they lived in tents on the mall near the Lincoln Memorial for a couple months one spring, during which time it poured down rain. But, the Congress clearly supported the USDA positions in expanding and improving the food programs.

*My Job*. My economist's position was set up directly under the Mr. Hekman. Previously, he had been President of Hekman Biscuit Company, a family business located in Kalamazoo Michigan, and more recently, he had been President of Kebler Biscuit Company. He appreciated the importance of having independent economic analysis within his office. He had four Special Assistants, with advisory responsibilities for general counsel (Peter Shambora), civil rights (Betty Dotson), political affairs (Mary Jane Fiske), and economics (myself). Philip Fleming was responsible for an Office of Public Information.

Hekman's Deputy Administrator for Operations was Howard Davis who had two Assistant Deputy Administrators, Isabelle Kelley and Marvin Sanstrom, initially. They had line responsibility for designing and operating all of the food programs. The Deputy Administrator for Administration was Arthur McCaw, and, later, Leonard Pouliot. Mr. Hekman tried to interest me in that job before Pouliot was hired but I told him I preferred doing the economic-oriented job that I had. Financially, that decision probably was a mistake because it would have been a grade raise to the GS-16 level, which I never did attain.

FNS had five regional offices, later expanded to seven,

with the job of working with the individual states in administering the programs at the local level. I worked closely with the operating divisions in Washington and often the regional offices in conducting or overseeing evaluation projects that often involved input from the respective programs. At that time, the five Regional Administrators were Chuck Ernst in the West at San Francisco; Martin Garber in the Southwest at Dallas; Wallace Warren in the Northeast at Princeton; Dennis Doyle in the Midwest at Chicago; and Russell James in the Southeast at Atlanta. They came to Washington (or met at other locations) for consultation with the Administrator quite often and I was usually invited to their meetings. They were dedicated to improving the programs, but they loved to play poker when they had some free time together, particularly Martin Garber.

It wasn't long, however, before my position was broadened to focus as much on policy analysis as it was on economic analysis. I was brought by Mr. Hekman into almost all major decisions related to restructuring of the food programs. I was asked to analyze the proposed changes and impacts of the final changes in laws or regulations that occurred almost every year during the early 1970s.

In addition, I had direct responsibility for making projections of the numbers of program recipients, the benefit levels that they received, and total budget requirements. Art Holmaas and later George Hall's budget division took my projections and worked out the financial details.

Due to our rapidly growing programs during the early 1970s, projecting budget needs was a major job. My staff and I developed a set of statistical models for the purpose. But, the programs kept evolving both by congressional action and by administrative decisions that made budget projections difficult. We often had to go back to the Congress with supplemental budget requests.

My position initially was set up with only a secretary to help me, but I quickly found the need for some help. I hired first one and then two assistants of my own, initially Dr. Orval Kerchner and Dr. J.C. Chai, both agricultural economists. Finally, I asked for funds to establish my own staff that we called the Economic Analysis and Program Evaluation Staff. This Staff grew to about 10-12 people over the years. After a couple years, Kerchner moved to another position and I hired Dr. Gar Forsht, another economist from ERS to take his place.

We were still not able to conduct a great deal of in-house research, but rather, concentrated on coordinating our own studies, and related work being conducted in one of our program divisions. As we saw the need to manage funded research programs, often under Congressional mandate, I was given a budget to conduct a number of studies under contract. That budget grew to about $2 million per year by the end of the decade.

I prepared an in-house report, *Program Evaluation Status Reports*, which we updated semi-annually for policy purposes. This report was in two parts, one summarized the status of studies currently underway and the second summarized the results of studies that had been completed by FNS (Hiemstra and Kerchner, 1973-78). Copies were distributed to the Directors of the Program Divisions and Staffs, the Regional Administrators, and the Child Nutrition Advisory Council *"For Official Use Only."*

I hired two other very good people, one was Emerson Hogentogler, (Hogey, as he was called) who was new in Government when I hired him, having been laid off as an economist from an aircraft company in San Diego, California when the industry there was downsizing. Later, when Guy Carmack retired, Hogey managed the Program Reporting Staff which collected and publicized all of the program data for FNS. The other person was Richard Platt, another economist. I hired Rich right out of graduate school from New Jersey. He not only stayed with me until I left FNS but stayed on later. He retired from FNS in 2007[2].

I had an unlimited travel budget to travel as much as I needed to or had time for; I took an average of about 17 trips per year working under Hekman, often giving speeches for him and overseeing various studies that we funded. I always tried to let Hekman know when I was traveling, but one time I failed to do so because he was unavailable. I was going down an escalator at the Atlanta airport when I met him coming up on the adjacent escalator. We were equally surprised to see each other, but he had no complaints at seeing me away from home. We did a lot of work with the Southeast Regional Office in Atlanta, particularly related to studies of the Child Nutrition Program (CNP), so I traveled there often.

*Mr. Hekman as Administrator.* Mr. Hekman was the finest boss that I ever had and ever would have. He was serious about management principles and tried to do things right. He brought his corporate mindset and many of his company procedures to Washington. One of the first things he did was to give each of us on his immediate staff a copy of Peter Drucker's book, *Management, Tasks, Responsibilities, and Practices* (1974). He often hired

---

[2] In recent years, he had been promoted to an Associate Administrator position in Financial Management and I am sure he did a good job. He is an expert on program accounting procedures and computer applications.

consultants to keep us up-to-date on current management practices. He was a believer in *Management by Objectives* and every year prevailed on all of the managers in his agency to develop goals and objectives for the coming year.

Mr. Hekman asked me to summarize the agency's objectives at the beginning of each year, by program, and to follow up by monitoring implementation as the year moved along. He and I, along with one or both of his Deputy Administrators, would visit each of our Regional Offices at Christmas time to bring them season's greetings and to engage them in presenting their goals and objectives for the coming year. Technically, this job was not within my job description but Mr. Hekman often gave me other additional duties. He regarded program evaluation as a broad mandate, but he also showed that he had a lot of personal trust in my judgment.

Hekman had a weekly meeting with his boss, Assistant Secretary of Agriculture Richard Lyng, who later became Secretary of Agriculture. He almost always took me along to those meetings as well as his two Deputy Administrators. I learned a lot about administration and the inside management of USDA and Washington in general at those meetings. I also worked very closely with Phillip Olson, who was Lyng's Deputy Assistant Secretary, in following up on decisions made at these meetings.

Mr. Hekman was very personable as well and knew a great many of his 1,800 rank and file employees by name. His door was always open to me. He told me to give him the straight facts as an economist and he would worry about the politics of my findings[3]. His, of course, was a Schedule C (political) position He recognized me as a career civil servant and purposely kept me out of the politics of his office. Mr. Hekman also was a strict disciplinarian, and a dedicated Lutheran. He expected his orders to be carried out, and promptly. I saw several people moved out or shunted aside who did not live up to his expectations. Fortunately, I was never one of them. He was quite respectful of his superiors and political figures, but he would not gloss over the truth as he knew it.

Mr. Hekman often talked publicly about his religion. One moving experience occurred when our FSP Director, Jim Kocker, committed suicide in the mid-1970s. His wife worked in the Child Nutrition Division, and she obviously was severely distraught by the incident. Apparently, it took her also completely by surprise. Of course, we all felt very badly about losing a colleague in this way with whom many of us worked on a daily ba-

---

3 This philosophy of management is known as logical positivism (Johnson 1986,42-50).

sis. Mr. Hekman held a moving memorial service for Jim in the administrator's conference room that he personally conducted.

In March 1975, I happened to be in Hekman's office the first thing one morning and we were both discussing a speech given the day before by the Secretary of the Treasury, William Simon. In that speech he was criticizing the FSP for being full of fraud and abuse, which was a common political theme at the time. The phone rang and Hekman took the call; Secretary Simon was on the line. Hekman put on his speakerphone so I could hear the conversation. He asked Hekman if he could find him some supporting documentation for the speech he had given the day before about the extensive fraud and abuse in food stamps. Hekman told him that, yes there was some fraud, but we had been studying it carefully and found it not to be excessive. In fact, I believe he told Secretary Simon that there probably was less fraud than he himself had in the IRS by people failing to pay their income taxes, which had been our finding. As his voice grew louder, Hekman told the Secretary that he would have no part in coming to his rescue, and he didn't. Nevertheless, Secretary Simon sent his statement to the Senate Select Committee on Nutrition and Human Needs.

*Additional Duties.* After a couple years, the Program Reporting Staff (PRS) was assigned to me as an additional duty. The PRS had the job of collecting and tabulating all of the program data and they prepared a detailed set of internal reports. Hogentogler remained in charge of the PRS. Later, my Staff was upgraded to a Division with Gar Forsht as Chief of one Branch and Hogentogler as Chief of the second Branch. We had about 25 people in total. My grade level remained at GS-15, at which I had been hired into FNS.

We also did a lot studies evaluating various aspects of the programs. There was no shortage of outside volunteers wanting to do research studies for FNS. Some of them had political overtones and some were simply looking for financial support. Unsolicited proposals often landed on my desk referred from Mr. Hekman's office. We quickly learned from our contract experts that we could only rarely fund sole source contracts without getting in trouble with the Office of Management and Budget (OMB).

The bulk of the studies that we funded needed to be designed in-house, formally bid, and then contracts given to the successful bidders. Going through the competitive bid process is very cumbersome, time consuming, and expensive. I worked closely in this effort with Vince Fowble and, later, Frank Gerard, director of our Management Services Division. But, the results were not always satisfactory.

We were constrained by the Government Procurement Regulations (A104) to hire the lowest priced bidders even if we did not think they were the most competent. I remember one contract specifically that we funded over my objections because it was the lowest bidder, only to find that they did not meet their commitments. They came back later asking for more money to finish the job, which we finally gave them, very reluctantly. It was a *"catch-22."* Had they asked for that much money initially, they would not have gotten the bid because they would not then have been the lowest bidder and I clearly did not regard their proposal as the best one submitted.

Partly because of the difficulties in contracting studies, early on I asked for help from ERS in conducting some of our needed studies. We signed a *Memorandum of Agreement* with ERS that was updated annually with specific studies. They were easier to manage than were outside contracts, and the ERS researchers were known to be competent. But, ERS was not able to do sizable jobs on this basis. I arranged such agreements in the range of $100,000 almost every year that I was in that position. After I left the agency, the Congress changed the legislation to give ERS funds directly to analyze the food programs.

Benefits under both FSP and CNP eventually were given escalators that were tied to changes in the Consumer Price Index (CPI). I was very much involved in the decisions about designing the appropriate escalators, and each year I had the job of calculating the actual levels of benefits that resulted. These escalators were key drivers in affecting the budget projections that we made annually and updated as needed for policy decisions or supplemental appropriation requests. Food stamp benefits were tied to the CPI for Food at Home and child nutrition benefits were tied to the CPI for Food Away From Home (upon my personal recommendation to the congressional committee in charge).

Two other important assignments that came my way over the years were more operational than economic in nature. They included: (1) setting up the Nutrition and Technical Services Staff of about 20 nutritionists, and managing it for one year till we could find a competent nutritionist as the staff director, and (2) chairing a four-man team which wrote the regulations for the WIC Program[4], and then managing that program during the first year of its operation when a permanent director was hired. As

---

4 WIC is an acronym for Supplemental Food Program for Women, Infants and Children.

additional duties, these were both sizeable jobs.

I consulted with many nutritionists in those days, including Dr. Fred Stare, head of the Nutrition Department at Harvard University. When he showed interest in our food programs, Hekman took me to Harvard University and introduced us.

## Food Stamp Program

*a. Program Policy Issues*

FSP was authorized by the Food Stamp Act of 1964 (U.S. Congress, 1964), however, it had been operating in pilot form in selected counties since 1961. The program legislatively had two primary objectives: (1) to increase the nutritional levels of low-income people, and (2) to increase the demand for farm food products. The program went through many modifications during the decade of the 1970s. The written objectives were not changed even though income redistribution became a third implicit objective when the purchase requirement was eliminated.

My concerns with FSP were mainly focused on assessing the program from the perspective of those two objects. However, I was also responsible for projecting program costs and participation for budget purposes, as well as costing out program efficiency and effectiveness alternatives from the standpoint of use of federal dollars. I am not a nutritionist but measuring food consumption and demand for food were subjects on which I had focused much attention for the previous decade. I also learned to work with nutritionists in designing and interpreting many food stamp studies of nutritional impacts.

By January 1971, the FSP had largely replaced the previous Food Distribution Program (FDP). It was generally conceded that the FDP was more designed to distribute surplus food commodities, and thereby increase the demand for farm commodities than to benefit the nutritional levels of the recipients. The food package donated did not provide a balanced diet, in part, because it was limited to nonperishable staple foods. One of key questions raised in the early 70s was whether food stamps or income donations would be better at delivering nutrition to low income people. As noted earlier, poor consumers' advocates strongly preferred cash donations rather than food programs, regardless of nutritional effectiveness. Clearly, they had little real interest in nutrition per se.

Even so, the FSP was initially designed by USDA to raise food consumption levels by requiring recipients to pay an amount for the stamps that they would nominally be expected to pay for their food. That was estimated to be 30 percent of income based on studies by USDA nutritionists. By requiring a purchase requirement, the extent to which the stamps donated exceeded this amount, the so-called bonus, would be expected to represent additional food spending.

There had been some early studies of the effectiveness of the pilot FSP, particularly one by Robert Reese in ERS (Reese,

Feaster and Perkins, 1974). This study estimated that about 45 percent of the food stamp bonus likely replaced personal food spending and therefore was spent indirectly on nonfood items. Those results were disturbing because they implied that less than half of the money spent on food stamps was being used for its intended purpose of increasing food spending.

The Congressional Budget Office (CBO, 1977) published another useful report evaluating the impacts of FSP. The CBO report focused strongly on their assessment that the purpose of the purchase requirement was to increase food expenditures, and they attempted to measure the extent to which the program provided indirect income supplementation. At that time, when the purchase requirement was still in effect, the report estimated that only 57 percent of the FSP bonus was being used for food and the remaining 43 percent substituted for personal food spending which represented income that was being used indirectly for nonfood purchases. Bill Hoagland, who had moved to CBO from FNS, was the primary author of this report.

This report pointed to the major changes in the program made in Food Stamp Act of 1971(U.S. Congress, 1971), including the increased benefits and national standards of eligibility implemented at that time. It noted that this Act required that recipients be given sufficient stamps to guarantee the opportunity to obtain a nutritionally adequate diet. This requirement was accomplished by tying the level of stamps provided to the level of the *"Economy Food Plan"* prior to January 1976. At this time, this food plan was renamed the *"Thrifty Food Plan"* but was defined the same and calculated by same people in ARS.

The FSP was designed to provide national standards of eligibility and benefit levels based almost solely on income (130 percent of the poverty level) and household size criteria rather than categorical eligibility of only certain types of people, as did welfare programs. At that time, welfare was given primarily to single mothers and their children. Prior to the 1971 Act, all FSP recipients received the same level of stamp issuance designed to meet nutritional adequacy as defined by the cost of the *Economy Food Plan*, toward which recipients contributed in relation to their income level (U. S. Congress, 1971). This so-called purchase requirement could not exceed 30 percent of income after allowance for several exemptions.

Poverty was defined by Mollie Orshansky (1965) as the level of income at which a household could purchase food at the level of the *Economy Food Plan*, as defined by ARS, USDA, by spending no more than thirty percent of their income. Mollie defined this concept for purposes of nutrition education, not for the uses for which it had become more widely applied in recent years, namely, for determining the eligibility for the various food assistance programs. In the early 1970s, the Government convened an interagency *Poverty Studies Task Force* to decide if the concept were properly defined for program purposes (Mahoney, 1977). I represented the interests of FNS on this Task Force, and Mollie was also a member. After a year or two of meetings and many white papers presented, no agreement could be reached for changing the definition, so it was left alone and remains intact to this day.

The definition of poverty turned mainly on the question of how to define income for purposes of the poverty definition, specifically, whether or not the income definition should continue to be based solely on cash-money income or whether the value of food assistance and other in-kind welfare benefits such as medical benefits under Medicaid and the Department of Housing and Urban Development's (HUD) Section 8 housing provided to low-income people should be included in the definition of income. Poverty levels for various household sizes continue to this day to be published annually by the U.S. Bureau of the Census. They are updated annually by percentage increases in the CPI, *All Items*.

Since the poverty definition is indexed for inflation and does not include food, medical, or housing assistance in calculating income, it is difficult for the number of people under poverty to ever decline because these forms of support are the primary means of Government efforts to help people get out of poverty (a tautology).

Since I was responsible for developing projections of FSP participation and costs, Rich Platt and I developed a set of statistical models to project the number of participants in FSP for budget purposes. After the program had been expanded to the national level, we found a close correlation between changes in unemployment and the number of FSP participants. Benefit levels were rather predictable once the escalators in benefits were tied to the CPI.

b. *Food Stamp Program Studies*

Several studies were conducted during the early to mid-1970s on the design, impacts and efficiency of the FSP, mostly funded by FNS and managed by myself or one of my staff. One of the first of these studies to evaluate the nutritional impacts of the FSP, was conducted in Pennsylvania under a contract that I negotiated and managed by Professor Pat Madden, Penn State

University (Madden and Yoder, 1972). It was completed in 1972, and was based in part on an M.S. thesis conducted by Bill Hoagland, who later came to work for me at FNS. Professors Sam Logan and Barton DeLoach at Berkeley conducted a further study of the FSP in two counties of Northern California (1973).

Professor Silvia Lane at the University of California at Davis also conducted a FSP study in two counties of Southern California focused on assessing nutritional impacts of the program. Her study had the help of Chris Ranney working on her Ph.D. dissertation (Lane, 1974). Ranney later became a professor and Dean at Cornell and continued to conduct studies of the FSP for several years. Results of these and related studies were included in the Program Evaluation Status Reports, discussed earlier.

Paul Nelson, my first boss in ERS as I mentioned in the previous chapter, conducted another study of the FSP as operated in Michigan supported by FNS under our cooperative agreement. It focused on the employment and unemployment relationships of recipients under the FSP, as well as the sales impacts of the FSP program on participating stores (1972). Nelson, working with Gar Forsht, later did a study of sales data collected by A.C. Nielson at automated supermarket checkout counters (which were new at that time) to compare the types of food purchased by food stamp recipients with that of cash food purchasers (Nelson, 1978).

Max Jordan and Msao Matsumoto in ERS also did an input-output analysis of the impacts of the FSP on local economies under this agreement (1971). Paul Nelson and John Perrin did a National study of the economic effects of both the FSP and the CNPs using input-output analysis (1976). It measured impacts on total business receipts, gross national product (GNP), and the increase in new jobs.

In March 1972, I had gone to Arizona and New Mexico to visit the Navajo Reservation for about two weeks to do a study to determine whether or not the Navajos should stay on the PDP[1], which had been providing them with food commodities, or switch to the FSP. It was well known that food prices were very high and food stores scarce, being located on isolated Indian trading posts with no competition among them. A complicating issue was the routine purchase of food and other supplies on credit at the trading posts. These credits presumably would be paid off during the harvest season. We visited six or eight trading posts in both New Mexico and Arizona and I surveyed the prices and availability of food offered for sale. We visited Window

---

1 PDP is a food distribution program.

Rock, and stayed at Farmington and Gallup, New Mexico.

Two representatives from the Southwest Regional Office accompanied me on this trip. One of them, Louis Gallegoes, was a Navajo Indian who worked for the FSP. He was helpful in introducing us at the trading posts that don't see too many white men asking questions. We concluded that a FSP probably could work there because food was generally more available than expected, and would clearly be more nutritious than the food commodities provided directly by the PDP. However, the program would need to be closely monitored relative to the credit indebtedness issue and concerns about fraud and abuse. The FSP later was initiated there.

The 1971 Amendments to the Food Stamp Act of 1964 extended the program to Puerto Rico, the Virgin Islands, Guam and the Northern Marianas, the latter three of which together constitute the U.S. Territories (Puerto Rico is defined as a Commonwealth). Up until this time, Puerto Rico and the Territories had received direct food commodity assistance from the U.S. About 600,000 people in Puerto Rico received food under this program, but they requested to be shifted to the FSP based on the new legislation.

I was given the job of working with Betty Peterkin and

the Southeast Regional Office in developing an Economy Food Plan for Puerto Rico and the Virgin Islands that could be used as the basis for FSP eligibility and benefit levels. That was a real job because income levels differed markedly and food consumption patterns in Puerto Rico were quite different from those in the U.S. Using the U.S. level of benefits would have meant that well over one-half of the 3-million population would have been eligible for benefits. The FNS budget was not adequate for this level of participation at the time. There were less than 6 million FSP participants in the entire U.S. in 1973.

Betty and I and a representative from our Atlanta office went to Puerto Rico in October 1973 to meet with their nutritionists and an Assistant to the Governor, Ramon Garcia Santiago, to develop a Thrift Food Plan to establish both the FSP eligibility and level of issuance. Initially, we met with strong resistance to our suggestions. I still remember the heated session we had with Santiago the day after we arrived in San Juan; Betty was particularly overwhelmed with the discussion. But, eventually, we had a meeting of the minds on an acceptable level of the Puerto Rico Economy Food Plan.

At our final meeting a few months later, Santiago hosted an all-day pig roast on a lovely beach to celebrate our agreements.

Even though the income level of eligibility for the FSP in Puerto Rico was set below that of the U.S., the average level of benefits in Puerto Rico exceeded that for the U.S. average. By 1976, per person benefits averaged $28.60 compared with $23.35 for the U.S. average, and participation exceeded 1 million persons. Several years later, however, the FSP was eliminated in Puerto Rico in favor of a cash subsidy.

After meeting with Santiago in Puerto Rico, Betty and I traveled to the Virgin Islands to work out an acceptable level of the Economy Food Plan for the Virgin Islands patterned after that in Puerto Rico. It only took a couple trips to accomplish an agreement.

Prior to implementation of the FSP in Puerto Rico, in July 1974 in some areas, we contracted with Professor Parimal Choudhury, University of Puerto Rico, to conduct a baseline study of food prices and types of purchases in three markets expected to be impacted by the program (Choudhury, 1975). The study was conducted in cooperation with the Department of Social Services as well as FNS. It measured incomes and developed estimates of household eligibility and participation levels. It was followed a year later by a second survey after the program had begun in those areas. It included sizable surveys of households, food retailers, and food wholesalers to assess the program's effects on food demand, food prices and the adequacy of the marketing system to supply the increases in demand (Choudhury, 1977).

This study showed a shift in demand for food from mainly rice, beans, poultry, and codfish to more preferred foods, such as beef, pork, and dairy products. Food expenditures increased by about 35 percent of the value of the bonus food stamps received (marginal propensity to consume food (MPC) = 0.35) and nonfood spending was up by 21 percent. This MPC of bonus food stamps at 0.35 is about in line with results from other food stamp studies; it much exceeds the normally expected MPC level of about 0.20 for cash income increases. Food prices rose by 8 percent, about in line with prices in areas not getting food stamps at the time. Food markets were able to handle the increase in demand without need for expansion due to previous overcapacity, for which we were grateful because we did not wish to adversely affect the economy.

Finally, a third study of the program's impact on employment was conducted because of concerns about the possible lack of employment incentives as a result of the widespread level of FSP participation (Choudhury, 1978). The study found that the unemployment rate actually had declined because food stamp recipients were less inclined to take part-time jobs and hold out for meaningful employment.

In October 1977, I went to Guam and Saipan, accompanied by a representative from our San Francisco Regional Office, to study the adequacy of the food markets there to support a FSP, as I had done earlier with the Navajo Nation. Guam was happy to continue on the Food Distribution Program (FDP) that they had had for many years, so we did not conduct a detail study there. We visited with the government officials in Guam, however, on our way to Saipan. They took us on a pleasant tour of the island and showed us some gun emplacements from World War II that still were in place on the northern tip of the island.

The Northern Marianas (mainly Saipan) wanted us to study the adequacy of the retail food market there in some detail. The main question was the adequacy of the food markets in Saipan to support a FSP without putting undue stress on prices. I conducted a survey of the food prices and visited most of their food stores in Saipan. The government officials were happy to see us and provided all of the information we needed. In the end, we recommended that Saipan remain on the FDP, at least for some time.

Saipan is a good-sized island, maybe 50-60 miles long, and an interesting place to visit. During out visit, we were shown some local sites made famous during the Japanes occupation during World War Two, including caves that were fortified and a high cliff on the north end of the island where many Japanese soldiers (and some civilians) jumped to their deaths as the U.S. Navy prepared to invade the island.

We also visited Rota, a small island off Saipan that is a part of Northern Marianas. Rota attained notoriety in World War II because it was from the airbase located there that the U.S. dropped the two atomic bombs on Japan. When I was there, the huge airstrip was still intact but largely unused. The island mainly hosted a large cattle ranch. It had only one food store and one restaurant on the island. There were very few people living there and they could easily commute the few miles to Saipan for shopping.

Senate Resolution 58 in 1975 called for USDA to do an extensive study of the FSP and I was very much involved in that effort. This Resolution was focused as much on reducing fraud and abuse of the program as it was on streamlining it to reduce its administrative complexities. These complexities were due in large part to piecemeal changes that had been made to increase income deductions from actual income of various kinds which served to increase benefit levels for certain categories of recipients. These included deductions for local, state, and federal taxes, high costs of shelter and medical costs, child care and education costs, disaster expenses, and work related expenses. FNS reported to Assistant Secretary Feltner at that time, and he presented the report to the Senate Agriculture Committee on October 7, 1975. (U.S. Congress, 1975a).

Secretary Feltner also had met with the Senate Select Committee on Nutrition and Human Needs in a food stamp hearing on this subject on July 31, 1975. It included Senators Dole and McGovern, both of whom were pleased with the report. The Congress published their own committee print containing many facts related to the program, which FNS provided (U.S. Senate, 1975b). Average monthly household gross income for a 4-person household averaged $238 in 1974. But, this level was reduced to $182 used for calculation of benefits after various deductions. U.S. bonus food stamps averaged $17.54 per person in 1974. Program costs totaled $5 billion in 1974, and served 17.3 million people in December 1974, including 1.5 million in

Puerto Rico.

Following these reports, the Congress approved legislation to allow a standard deduction in lieu of some of the many previous income deductions to reduce the complexity and time needed to certify participants. They also agreed to change certain administrative procedures to reduce perceived fraud and abuse. FNS reported that approximately 0.08 percent of the average monthly participation was found to be participating on a fraudulent basis in fiscal year 1974 (U.S. Senate, 1975b, p. 18), which the agency did not regard as excessive.

One proposed study on which I spent a lot of time and effort (beginning in 1974), never did get approval of the OMB, a prerequisite to spending money on a large study. It was to be a nationally-representative panel survey of low-income households continued over at least a two-year period of time to track the same people as they moved on and off of various food assistance programs. I had convened a blue-ribbon panel of 6 or 7 statistical and nutrition experts that developed the study's specifications and the formal request for proposals (RFP). Program impacts would be measured on the adequacy of their diets and comparisons made before and after program participation giving dietary as well as rates of participation of those eligible. I had secured $1 million for the study and it had been approved by FNS and the Secretary of Agriculture's office. OMB felt that a new Household Food Consumption Survey (HFCS) by ARS could provide much of the information needed. It turned out that the HFCS was never approved, and such data have never been collected.

Consumer advocates very much liked the design of the FSP and the national standards of eligibility based on income of the revised program. But, as mentioned, they considered as onerous the requirement under the program at the time that recipients had to pay 30 percent of their net income to get the stamps. In other words, they did not want to give food demand preference over demand for nonfood products, even though that preference was an objective of the legislation. Recipients received stamps in proportion to their family size and level of the Thrifty Food Plan.

After much debate on the merits and economic effects of the change, the eligibility purchase requirement (EPR) was eliminated from the FSP in January 1979, as a result of passage of the Food and Agricultural Act of 1977 (U. S. Congress, 1977). EPR was strongly recommended by the new administration because they put increasing program participation ahead of the objective of improving nutritional impacts. Regulations implementing the change were issued October 17, 1978 requiring the changes as of January 1979.

The level of stamps provided to individual recipients was reduced by nearly one-half as a result of EPR even though Government costs were largely unchanged. Nutritional benefits from the program were expected to be reduced because there was no longer any requirement for recipients to use any of their own income for food, as previously. But, there was a substantial increase in FSP participation because recipients often had trouble coming up with the purchase requirements.

As a result, I felt that the program was given a third major objective, that of income redistribution per se (Hiemstra, 1976). Others regard the program as a form of negative income tax, even before EPR (Nathan, 1976). Nathan regarded food stamps as a stepping-stone to welfare reform, which I thought was appropriate and I wrote an article supporting the idea.

Other changes made by the 1977 Act tightened the eligibility criteria. Eligibility was limited to the poverty level whereas previously it had been determined by the level of benefits reaching zero based on the 30 percent of income criteria, which yielded a higher level. Deductions to income were also reduced and the work requirement was made more stringent. Categorical eligibility for Aid to Families with Dependent Children (AFDC) and social security insurance (SSI) recipients was eliminated, as were students who were tax dependents of an ineligible household. The 1979 and 1980 Amendments further tightened eligibility in attempts to reduce fraud and abuse. Even so, increasing participation due to EPR's impact overshadowed the impacts of these restrictions. Participation totaled 15.4 million persons in December 1978, the last month prior to EPR. A year later, participation had risen to 20. 1 million and it reached 22 million in August 1980.

However, these increases were not all due to EPR because participation was stimulated by the adverse economic conditions at the time. Inflation was rampant and unemployment levels surging from 5.8 to 7.4 percent. The percentage of participants receiving public assistance declined from 48 percent in November 1978 to 42 percent 12 months later as a result.

Some later studies showed that nutritional benefits from the program continued to be measurably larger than they would have been under an income supplement alone. Using data from the 1979-80 *Survey of Food Consumption of Low-Income People*, Devaney and Moffitt developed a statistical model of levels of 10 individual nutrients plus energy consumed related to food stamp benefits and income levels (1990). It showed that food stamp benefits provided more nutritional impacts than did comparable income levels. The purchase requirement had been eliminated just before the time of this survey. Presumably, just getting food stamps entices people to continue to use more of their resources (money plus stamps) for food than they would without the stamps, even though they are not required to do so.

Aside from a continuing focus on nutrition in ever broadening studies, increasing attention was given to assessing the extent to which the FSP was reaching its target audience of low-income people. Participation rates before the purchase requirement was eliminated were estimated to be in the range of 40-45 percent of those eligible (Beebout, 1978). But after its elimination, participation rates climbed quickly to about 60-65 percent in the 1980s (Allin, Beebout, Doyle, and Trippe, 1990). Participation was particularly high among women receiving welfare (AFDC). Those unemployed also participated at relative high rates. This segment is more variable than in the case of AFDC participants, which makes variation in unemployment useful in projection models.

FNS developed a FSP microsimulation model with the help of Mathematica Policy Research (Beebout, 1978). It was called Transfer Income Model (TRIM), based in part on annual program participation surveys of participants conducted annually by the Food Stamp Division, as well as use of the 1967 Survey of Economic Opportunity Census' annual Consumer Population Survey that was used to update the Office of Economic Opportunity (OEO) data. This model provided the necessary parameters to estimate the effects of legislative program changes and various proposed changes.

## Child Nutrition Programs

*Legislation and Organization.* The objectives of the National School Lunch Act (NSLA) are *"to safeguard the health and well-being of the Nation's children and to encourage the domestic consumption of nutritious agricultural commodities and other food"* (U.S. Congress, 1946). NSLA responded to the shocking experiences of the military in having to reject a significant percentage of draftees whose poor health was linked to poor nutrition as children. Since the Great Depression, USDA had provided surplus food to the schools to support agricultural prices by stimulating food demand. Now, the NSLA, as amended, added a second objective of increasing domestic food consumption. In view of both concerns, the donation of physical commodities to schools continues to be an important program.

The Child Nutrition Programs (CNP) include the NSLP but also the School Breakfast Program (SBP), the Child Care Foodservice Programs (CCFP), and several direct food distribution programs. At one time the Special Milk Program (SMP) was large, but by the mid-1970s was almost entirely supplanted by NSLP, which includes milk. The NSLP requires that a nutritionally adequate diet be served in the schools in order to qualify for the Federal assistance provided. This diet was early on labeled a

"Type A" meal pattern and until the 1980s consisted of 2 ounces of meat (or a meat-like product), a portion of a cup of two or more vegetables, a slice of bread, and a half-pint of milk (for elementary schools). These foods are expected to provide about one-third of the RDA for school age children.

The SBP was authorized by the Child Nutrition Act of 1966 as a pilot program to provide breakfasts in schools in low-income districts whose children had to travel long distances to school (U.S. Congress, 1966). They had to offer free breakfasts to poor children and paid breakfasts to other children in areas with a program. In 1975, the program was authorized nationally but most meals continued to be served free to children. Children from households with incomes below 130 percent of poverty were entitled to free breakfasts and those from households between 130 and 185 percent of poverty were entitled to reduced price breakfasts.

The meal requirement for breakfast initially consisted of one serving each of milk, fruit or vegetable juice, and bread or cereal. These foods are expected to provide one-fourth of the RDA for school age children. The Child Nutrition Act of 1998 authorized serving free breakfasts to all children in six pilot areas for three years because of feeling that breakfasts are extremely important nutritionally for all school children. Many of them are known to skip breakfasts regardless of income level.

Child Care Food Programs (CCFP) consisted initially of two target groups of low-income school children: (1) a summer feeding program to provide food while children were not in school, and (2) preschool children in day-care centers or other nonresidential child care settings. The CCFP were authorized under section 17 of the National School Lunch Act. Funds were provided to state educational agencies for distribution to public and private nonprofit organizations. In 1975, P.L. 94-105 expanded the CCFP programs to provide assistance to family day care, Head Start centers, and residential child-care centers (RCCI's). As you see, these programs were just developing during the 1970s.

At the time FNS was formed in 1969, grants in support of the NSLP were given to the states on the basis of the number of students being served the previous year and the income level of the state in relation to national income. They were required to provide meals free to children from low-income households as a condition for receiving federal assistance, but relatively little additional funding was made available for this purpose. This system did not perform well because there was no incentive to increase the number of free price meals. In fact, it hurt the overall program because the federal assistance was quite low relative to the cost of serving the free meals.

Since 1946, the federal assistance was partly in the form of cash and partly in the form of commodities. Before that time, commodities constituted the only federal assistance given to schools, under Section 32 of the Agricultural Marketing Act. These commodities were purchased primarily to remove surplus products from agricultural markets. But, under Section 6 of NSLA, commodities were purchased specifically to meet the food preferences of the schools.

Public Law (P.L.) 91-248 was passed in 1970, soon after the formation of FNS, to amend the NSLA to strengthen the programs and to fund federal reimbursements on a performance basis. Section 4 of the NSLA initially provided basic support of 6 cents in cash for every meal served; section 6 provided a like amount in value of preferred commodities for every meal. Section 11 was amended by PL 91-248 to provide that all children from households below 100 percent of the poverty level ($3,720 for a 4-person household at the time) were to be served lunch free or at a reduced price.

A year later, the income limits were liberalized to 125

percent of poverty for free meals ($5,140) and between 125 and 175 percent of poverty ($5,141-$6,160) for reduced price meals. Free and reduced price meals were reimbursed at 40 cents plus the basic rate of 6 cents cash and 6 cents worth of commodities. Student meals eligible for reduced price meals were charged about 20 cents. At this time, the cost of producing a school lunch was about 60 cents. These federal reimbursement rates on a per-meal-served-basis were a big step forward in the war on poverty, and I had an important role in making the changes in funding a reality.

In fiscal year (FY) 1973, the NSLA was again amended to provide that reimbursement rates be routinely escalated semi-annually so they would increase at the same rate as prices in the CPI. One day when this legislation was in final stages of being passed, I got a call from a staff member on the House Education and Labor Committee who was "marking up" (finalizing) the final version of the bill and I was asked which CPI would be the most appropriate for escalating child nutrition benefits over time. I had analyzed this very question, comparing trends in various food price indexes to known increases in costs of producing a school lunch, which we had at that time.

I told the caller about my studies on this question and

recommended that the Food Away From Home component of the CPI be used as the escalator. The staff person on the Committee inserted this index into the legislation without further debate, and the change passed into law in that form. It has been there ever since. That is how many fine points of legislation get decided in Washington. *"The devil is in the details."*

Various attempts have been made over the years for all school meals to be served free, but sufficient funds have never been available for this purpose. The American School Food Service Association (ASFSA) has been the primary proponent of this request. I was asked many times to estimate the costs of providing free lunches and breakfasts for all children; the program costs would about triple.

There are two geographic areas, however, that had always served free meals to all elementary school children: Puerto Rico and the Virgin Islands. These meals traditionally had been paid for by their government. In this case, surveys were conducted periodically during the 1970s and 1980s to determine the percentage of students from low-income households that would qualify for free or reduced price meals. That percentage is the basis for the reimbursement rates paid by FNS. I traveled to Puerto Rico and the Virgin Islands annually in the mid to late 1970s to set up and design the necessary surveys. Program eligibility levels were the same in Puerto Rico and the Virgin Islands as in the U.S. so most of the meals were reimbursed by FNS.

Eligibility levels are 10 percent higher in Hawaii and 25 percent higher in Alaska than in the 48 contiguous states. The reason is that their food prices and income levels are generally higher than in the 48 states, but I am not sure how FNS derived those particular numbers. I never studied them.

Because of the integral part played by nutrition in all of the food assistance programs, we decided in 1970 that we should have a separate organization composed of nutritionists within FNS to do nutrition analysis and make appropriate nutritional decisions. Mr. Hekman asked me to organize such an organization. We called it the Nutrition and Technical Services Staff (NTSS) and it later was upgraded to Nutrition and Technical Services Division (NTSD). I served as the Acting Director of NTSS, as an additional duty, for one year until we could find a competent nutritionist to manage the program. Prior to this time, there were a few nutritionists in the Child Nutrition Division so they were transferred to the new Staff to serve as its nucleus. That turned out to be an important decision because nutritional issues later became an increasing concern of FNS. Dr.

Dan Rosenfield became the Director of NTSS in 1972, followed by Dr. Grace Ostenso about a year later.

*The Rutgers Study.* One of the first studies of the CNPs that we launched after the inception of FNS, in March 1970, was an in-depth analysis of new foods that could be served under the CNP to make them nutritionally improved, more efficient, and help to stimulate program participation (Department of Food Science, 1972). Hopefully, the new foods would be tasty and help to increase program participation. We entered into a contract with the Food Science Department of Rutgers University for this purpose. I was designated to be the contracting officer's representative (COR) for the study, because of my association with NTSS, and Dr. Paul LaChance who was the Principal Investigator at Rutgers. He had been heavily involved in developing foods used by the astronauts on their various space missions. They were to study various products available from the food industry as well as possibly develop new product themselves.

Once the word circulated in industry groups, we, as well as Rutgers, became inundated with proposed new food offerings. We directed almost all such inquiries to the Rutgers group. They studied hundreds of different products. However, Mr. Hekman was invited to St. Louis to view an important new food product that showed promise. He invited me along on this trip. We were shown a product that later turned out to be Pringles potato chips, or something very similar. We also visited General Food's laboratories in White Plains, New York for the same purpose. I don't remember the particular products they were promoting, but I do remember the fancy limousine that met us at the airport and took Mr. Hekman and me to their property.

Out of this study emerged three products that we approved for use in our programs. One was a chocolate breakfast cake that contained a nutritious, tasty filling, not too dissimilar from Twinkies. The second was a fortified macaroni for use in the NSLP. These two products met the nutrient requirements of our programs, and they were rather well accepted by the schools, at least for a time. Nutritionists, however, were skeptical of the sugar and fat contents of the breakfast cake. I don't know if they were commercially successful or not.

The third product was textured vegetable protein (TVP) for use as a substitute for some of the ground beef used in hamburger patties and related products like chili and sloppy-joe sandwiches. We allowed up to 30 percent of the finished product to consist of TVP. Our taste tests showed that when no more than 30 percent of TVP was used that one could not taste the difference. The advantages were that TVP was composed of soybean protein that resulted in a much higher percentage of protein and less animal fat in the end product. It was also less expensive than 100-percent meat.

This product was approved for use in NSLP by NTSS when I was the Acting Director. It was extensively used in school lunch programs, and perhaps is still being used. We launched a new food that likely was profitable to both the schools and the food industry. The downside was that schools sometimes exceeded the 30 percent limitation, and thereby served products that tended to be dry and tasteless. The product was highly touted by an Assistant to the Secretary of Agriculture, Dr. Aaron Altshsult, a food technologist who later became a professor at Georgetown University.[1]

In summary, the Rutgers study was rather disappointing. It had some successes, such as TVP, but it was costly and took a lot of my time. I traveled there several times to review the findings and guide the study, but the final report, although voluminous, was late in arriving and did not live up to my expectations. It consisted mostly of a one-by-one appraisal of the many prod-

---

[1] Dr. Aaron Altshsult and Dr. Carol Luhrs, an M.D. who also was an Assistant to the Secretary, once traveled with me to Puerto Rico to review the programs.

ucts that they tested without useful summary or recommendations. I wrote a critical appraisal of it that I sent to the Head of the Rutgers Food Science Department.

*The Washington State Study.* In 1970, we decided to conduct an in-depth analysis of the school lunch and breakfast programs. We awarded a contract to Washington State University to draw random samples of students in various part of that state for dietary, food acceptance, nutritional, biochemical, economic, and sociological evaluations. Data were collected from 728 students from representative 8 to 12 year age groups, and three ethnic groups (white, black and Hispanic). The study also compared lunch and breakfast participants with non-participants and looked at FSP participation.

There was a large team of researchers involved in this study, under the Co-Chairmanship of Dr. Margaret Ward, Dean of the School of Nutrition, and David Price, an agricultural economist. I personally monitored this study carefully, and visited Pullman three or four times to get updates and results of this three-year study. A wide range of findings resulted from this comprehensive study (Price, Hard, et al, 1976, and Price, West, Scheier, and Price 1979).

Donald West, an agricultural economist who participated in the Washington State Study measured the price elasticity of demand for school lunches. It was calculated from the price and participation data collected from the state to determine how price-sensitive students are in purchasing lunches at school. They found that, on average, an increase in price of 10 percent resulted in a drop in participation of 4 to 6 percent (West and Hoppe, 1973). The price elasticity was higher for relatively small districts than for the larger districts. They also found that there was on average a drop of 1 paid recipient for every increase of 4 students receiving free lunches. Don later came to Washington for one year as a visiting professor and worked with my staff and me on related studies.

*One-Percent Authorities.* P.L 91-248 had another provision that very much affected me directly. Section 6(a)(3) provided that up to 1 percent of the program funds provided to the states under NSLA of 1946 and CNA of 1966 could be used *"for nutrition education and training projects for workers and for necessary studies and surveys"* (U.S. Congress, 1970). We encouraged the states to use this provision to fund child nutrition education and training efforts as well as various studies. However, the regulations required that these efforts be individually approved by FNS to ensure quality studies and lack of duplication of efforts in use of these funds. I had the job of working with many states on these efforts, which often involved travel to the states or regional offices involved. We encouraged cooperative efforts within the regions. Many of them conducted region-wide seminars, some of which I attended. Another such study, in which I was personally involved because it was an economic analysis, was a five-county project in Florida focused on seeking economies in purchasing by buying their food supplies cooperatively.

Some states, universities, and regional offices were much more actively involved in promoting these research and educational efforts than others. They included Georgia (Josephine Martin, State School Lunch Director), Florida (Thelma Flanegan, State Director), Kansas (Professor Allene Vaden, Kansas State University), and California (Jean White, School Lunch Director). The Southeast regional office under their Child Nutrition Director Bill Griffeth and his assistant Nena Bratiano, were much more actively involved in promoting these efforts than the other regional offices. Josephine Martin, who later became President of ASFSA, was very active in promoting research and education efforts, as well as actively engaged with FNS on policy issues. I worked closely with her on many projects.

*Comprehensive Study of Child Nutrition Program.* In 1974,

I had responsibility for putting together a detailed compilation and analysis of the CNP. It was sent to the Senate Committee on Agriculture and Forestry that published it as a Committee Print, entitled, *Comprehensive Study of the Child Nutrition Programs* July 1974. It contained 37 tables and 87 pages of information. The major sections of the report included the following:

    I. Purpose of the study

    II. Child nutrition program benefits

    III. Trends affecting the programs

    IV. Program participation

    V. Federal-state programs costs of administration

    VI. Cost variations between regions and states

    VII. Program alternatives

    VIII. Other programs available

    IX. Recommendations and conclusions

My office wrote major sections of the report, such as program benefits, trends affecting the programs, and costs of the various program alternatives. The program divisions outlined the historical details of the programs, and NTSD focused on the nutritional aspects. The alternative of a universal free lunch was expected to increase participation from 25 to 36 million children (90 percent of the total attendees) and to increase Federal costs from $1.2 billion to $3.3 billion, at FY 1973 levels. Costs of producing a school lunch were estimated at 76 cents per meal at that time.

*Research Review*. In 1976, Professor Allene Vaden established an Editorial Policy Board to establish a refereed journal exclusively for publishing child nutrition research. I met with the Board in February 1977 in Manhattan, Kansas to help establish the goals and objects of the Research Review. It was called the School Foodservice Research Review, to be published semi-annually by ASFSA beginning in 1977. I was invited to be a consultant to the Board. Allene Vaden was a very active researcher in the nutrition department at Kansas State and had conducted considerable research on school lunch, along with her students.

I remained a consultant to the Research Review as long as I was with FNS and then became an active member of the Advisory Board until 1996. By then, Allene Vaden had moved to the University of Southern Mississippi as Dean of Nutrition and had died (in 1987), while I was at Purdue University. I continued to do research related to school food service programs all the time I was at Purdue and published many articles in the Research Review. In fact, I was invited to join Purdue University because of my contacts on the Advisory Board of the Research Review. In 1998, the name of the journal was changed to The Journal of Child Nutrition & Management. I am sure that Allene would not have agreed to this change because the purpose of the journal was thereby shifted to management rather than research which had been strongly fostered by Allene.

Between 1979 and 1996, I published nine special articles in the Research Review, four of them while I was still at FNS and five while at Purdue. The articles I published while at FNS covered the subjects of

1. *"Cash in Lieu of Commodities in School Food Service Programs"* (Hiemstra, 1979),

2. *"Economic Importance of the National School Lunch Program"* (Hiemstra, 1979),

3. *"Impacts of the Omnibus Budget Reconciliation Act of 1981"* (Hiemstra, 1982), and

4. *"National School Lunch Program Trends"* (Hiemstra, 1983a).

In addition, beginning in 1983 I published a 4 or 5 page regular feature in the Research Review entitled *"Program Data and Analysis,"* which summarized and discussed trends in CNP data (total of 21 issues).

*Computer Assisted Menu Planning.* As early as 1970, we became concerned that the NSLP meal pattern was too restrictive in terms of defining a nutritionally adequate diet. Many foods other than those specified in the Type A pattern might provide important nutrients and if so they should also count toward the requirement. Many schools particularly those serving various ethnic groups were clamoring for some flexibility in the food requirement. Many of these specific requests were handled administratively on a case-by-case basis. Pressure developed to broaden the concept of a nutritionally adequate diet redefined in terms of nutrients rather than in terms of food groups, and to allow the computations to be computerized. But, there was opposition to this concept because many school lunch directors were dieticians but not professionally trained nutritionists, and few of them had the requisite computer skills. This debate raged on for many years and several tests were conducted to find a system that could satisfy both sides of the issue.

We funded some researchers at Tulane University in 1971 to conduct a study of Computer Assisted Menu Planning (CAMP). We contracted with Management Optimization Systems, Inc. to code menu data from our USDA school lunch recipes and modify computer program specifications to allow computerized menu planning. We also supported some of the states in comparing nutritional results of menu planning using computers with the traditional meal planning based on Type A requirements, working with Fred Shank, NTSD (Tennessee Department of Education, 1975 and Florida Department of Education, 1975). The issue was not resolved until the mid- 1980s after I had moved to Purdue University when nutrient standard menu planning (NSMP) became required by USDA. See my chapter on Purdue University.

This issue took some strange twists and turns. One of them was related to ketchup. It was noted that ketchup is made from tomatoes so the nutrients in ketchup should count in part toward the vegetable requirement. This case became a political issue when some consumer activists pointed out publicly that FNS was calling ketchup a vegetable and thereby denigrating the school lunch program. This situation occurred in about 1981 after President Carter had been replaced by President Reagan. At that time, Bill Hoagland had been recalled from his staff position with the U.S. Congress and elevated to serve as the Administrator of FNS. The issue became so elevated that Hoagland was asked to leave his job. He returned to the Budget Committee of the Congress where he remains today in a high-level position.

*Child Nutrition Review.* In 1977, I was again involved in preparing a comprehensive evaluation of the CNP. This study included the WIC program as well, in part because it was funded under the NSLA. We bound and printed this report, Child Nutrition Review, and distributed it widely in-house for policy purposes as well as sent copies to the Congress. Part I A of the report focused on the CNPs was 130 pages long and contained 59 tables (Hiemstra, 1978). It included the following major sections:

1. Overview of the Programs

2. Factors affecting participation and costs

3. Profile of participants and type of food service

4. Nutritional aspects of the programs

5. Economic impacts of the programs

6. Relationship to other programs.

Part II of the report was prepared by the Child Nutrition Division and focused on programmatic concerns such as administration details and the handling of commodities.

This report included details of a separate study that had been conducted of the administrative costs that the CNPs imposed on the state agencies that administered the program in the various states, mandated by P.L. 94- 105. FNS had always provided some funds to the states to cover their costs, but many states felt that those funds were not covering an adequate share of the total costs of administration. I assisted in conducting that study as well, which involved a detailed survey of all states and personal visits to many of them. Annual state costs were estimated at $22.7 million, of which FNS paid $5.2 million.

A second, earlier study focused on measuring costs that the states incurred by managing the food distributed under the School Lunch Program. We contracted with AT Kearney, Inc., management consultants, to do this study, which I managed (1974). The weighted, average cost of state and local distribution of the foods provided for the schools came to 5.3 cents per meal served. This included warehousing, transportation and administration. Local recipient agencies paid 61 percent of these costs and the states contributed the remaining 39 percent. We circulated this report to the states and I think it was the last time we heard their complaints about these costs being burdensome. In 1973, federal cash reimbursements totaled 82 cents per meal so these costs amounted to only 6 percent of the total.[2]

The Child Nutrition Review also reviewed the literature on national surveys of nutrition that measured nutrient deficiencies of school age children. These included most notably

> 1. The 1971 HANES survey conducted by the National Center for Health Statistics, (1975),
>
> 2. The USDA's 1965-66 Household Food Consump-

---

[2] Editor's note: 5.3 divided by 82 is 6.4 percent.

tion Survey (1972), and

3. The DHEW Ten State Survey conducted in 1968-70 (1970).

These surveys highlighted the deficiency primarily of iron in diets of low-income school-age children.

The report also highlighted the results of several nutritionally-oriented school lunch studies, including the Washington State University study cited above (Price, 1976), the Head study in North Carolina funded by FNS (1975), and the Colorado State survey funded by FNS (Harper and Jansen, 1973), all of which I was much involved in designing and managing. It also highlighted the 80,000-student Massachusetts study by John Stalker (State School Lunch Director) funded by their state Department of Education (1972). Stalker's study was often cited in showing the superiority of the NSLP school lunches over bag lunches sent from home. This report also cited the studies we had conducted of computer assisted menu planning, discussed previously.

Part I A of the report also noted some studies of food preferences and plate waste that we funded. These efforts resulted in approving the *"offer versus serve"* provision in the program designed to reduce undue food waste. Under that provision, students do not need to take food that they do not plan to eat, as had been the case when food was required to be served to justify federal reimbursements.

## Child Care Food Service

*M*y office conducted a two-phased study of the meal quality and program costs of the Summer Food Service Program, which was mandated by P.L. 94-105 (Litschauer, 1978). John Litschauer, who was on my staff, worked with Henry Rodriguez, Director of the Child Care and Summer Program Division and the regional offices to collect the necessary survey data. In this connection, I visited a summer feeding program operating in New York during its formative period. These programs were difficult to manage unless operated in association with a school foodservice program. Means tests are difficult to administer for purposes of eligibility for these programs. In 1982, however, income eligibility was established at 125-130 percent of poverty for free meals and 185-195 percent of poverty for reduced price meals (Abt Associates, 1988).

*Food Price and Cost Studies.* Gar Forsht worked with Paul Nelson in ERS in conducting a survey of prices paid by individual school districts in comparison with prices paid for the same food items purchased nationally by USDA (ERS, 1974). The intent was to measure economies of scale in purchasing foods by different sized districts in contrast with prices paid by USDA. The survey was based on 15 specified common foods used by the schools. The universe was 150 school districts stratified into three size groups. We found that USDA paid virtually the same prices as did the largest-sized school districts, but they both paid 18 percent less than did the smallest-sized districts.

We also did several studies to determine if cooperative buying by groups of schools or districts saved much money over doing it independently. Usually, groups could buy food more cheaply because of their larger sizes but offsetting factors such as the need for uniformity in specifications and inventory costs when buying in large volume offset some of the advantages. It also required experienced buyers to be effective.

As an economist, I have always been interested in measuring variations in prices and levels of costs. Later, when I was at Purdue University, one summer I conducted an extensive study of food costs in Indiana schools, and the factors associated with varying costs such as size and locations of school districts within the state. I did much of the surveying myself, but I had a graduate student to help. Between us, we surveyed a random sample of over 80 school districts.

John Litschauer later conducted a cost-economies of scale study for producing type A lunches based on three simulated, alternative types of program operations. These included on-site, base-satellite, and central operations (Litschauer and Canevello, 1977).

### Women, Infant, and Children Program[1]

The Special Supplemental Food Program called WIC was established by P.L. 92-433 on September 26, 1972. The enabling legislation amended the Child Nutrition Act as Section 17. It authorized a 2-year pilot program to provide supplemental foods to pregnant, post-partum, and breastfeeding women, infants and children up to four years of age who are at nutritional risk because of inadequate nutrition and income. WIC's mandate was to function as an *"adjunct to good health care,"* and for that reason the program was set up to be administered through state health organizations funded by the Secretary of Agriculture, rather than state welfare organizations as was the FSP.

The program was given the acronym, WIC (which I coined, as the first director of the program) because the department already had a Supplemental Food Program that had been serving the same clientele for a few years, primarily by direct distribution of commodities. And, we even had a second similar program called the Food Certificate Program operating in two areas, South-side Chicago and Bibb County Georgia since 1970. It provided $5 certificates each month to pregnant women until delivery and then $15 certificates monthly for each infant for 12 months. We had conducted a formal evaluation of that program

---
1 http://www.fns.usda.gov/wic/women-infants-and-children-wic.

in April 1971. I had personally visited the program operating in Chicago and designed the evaluation that was contracted with Cornell University (Wunderle and Call, 1971). But, the Congress wanted a new program.

I was asked by the administrator to head a 4-person task force to develop the regulations for the WIC program on a crash basis, and to serve as the Acting Director of the program for one year. I hired two medical doctors as consultants to help us design the program appropriately from a medical perspective. One was Doctor Fomen, a pediatrician from the University of Iowa medical school. Implementation began in mid-1973 with the selection of project sites. By January 1974 we had 24 sites operating that were serving 709 people. By the end of the year we had 255 sites operating with an approved caseload of 402,000, and the budget had been expanded to $100 million for FY 1975 from the $20 million authorized for the pilot program. Everyone seemed to like the program so it never went out of existence. Many commentators have said it is the best food program available. Today, the program is national in scope with an annual budget exceeding $4 billion.

For my efforts in getting the program established, I was once introduced, in jest, as *"the father of the WIC program"*. I was in Boston at the time giving a talk to the FNS program staff and was introduced by their regional administrator, Harold McLean. By coincidence, he ended up as director of the WIC Program in Washington a couple years later.

WIC recipients were provided with vouchers or coupons redeemable at local food stores. They could be used for milk, cheese, eggs, cereal, and juices. Soon, infant formula could be substituted for the milk for infants but milk was still provided for the women. Alternatively, local areas could provide the physical food products directly rather than provide for vouchers or coupons, but this option has not been widely used. The local health clinic was also required to provide nutrition education to recipients. The health clinics liked the program because it provided an incentive for low-income recipients to come into the clinics for health care whereas they otherwise may be reluctant to do so.

A second unique feature of the program, aside from operating through health clinics, was that a medical evaluation of the health benefits to recipients of the program was mandated in the Regulations. Our first evaluation was set up immediately by contract with the University of North Carolina at Chapel Hill under Dr. J.C. Edozien. His first report, in two large volumes, was dated July 15, 1976 (Edozien, Switzer, and Bryan, 1976).

The conclusions from the Edozien study were quite positive for the WIC program. The measurements were taken before recipients participated in the program and after they moved off of the program. It showed:

> 1. Program participation was associated with an increase in weight and height of infants and children;
>
> 2. Head circumference was found to be increased if the infants enrolled within one month of birth;
>
> 3. There was a consistent increase in mean blood hemoglobin concentration of all participating infants, children, and women;
>
> 4. Women also showed a reduction in rates of anemia when pregnant for 24-31 weeks of participation;
>
> 5. Pregnant women who participated in the program gained more weight during pregnancy than did women in the initial population;
>
> 6. There was an increase in mean birth weights for participating babies, particularly for Hispanic and black babies.

In 1977, FNS did their own evaluation of the program and several other studies have been conducted since that time.

One of the concerns of Mr. Hekman was that there was considerable overlap in benefits of the FSP and the WIC program. Infants and young children served by WIC also were (and still are) entitled to receive a full measure of stamps equivalent to that given to adults. About half of the WIC recipients have also received food stamps over the years. I have never understood why an infant had any use for a full allotment of food stamps while also getting infant formula and other foods under WIC. Such benefit overlaps are likely the cause of observed waste in food assistance programs, and could easily be removed.

### Personal Travel

*M*exico. In January 1971, I took a week-long personal trip with my two brothers to Mexico. I met John and David in Dallas, following one of my trips to our Dallas regional office. John, an RCA pastor, needed to take a business trip to Chiapas in southern Mexico, near Guatemala. John had his own plane that he often flew on business trips and was planning to fly down to San Cristóbal de las Casas in the province of Chiapas. He had responsibility at that time for overseeing the church's mission programs in the U.S. and Mexico and he had to go there for some meetings. He asked Dave and I to accompany him there just for the ride, and we accepted. After the meetings, we vacationed a few days in Acapulco and Mexico City. He was flying a single-engine *"Mooney"* that had room for four people.

Our trip had its ups and downs, literally. On our first night in Mexico, we flew south from Dallas a couple hundred miles but found the airport closed. Fortunately, they had left the lights on for us so we landed without incident. But, it was a bit eerie going into an airport with no people to greet you, especially because we were in a foreign country that normally requires people to clear customs before going into town. After some searching, we did find a night watchman who assured us that we could return in the morning to clear customs. That's what we did, with no problems. The next day we flew to San Cristóbal. I did wonder if John could always understand the broken English used by the air traffic controllers, but he managed. It was probably better than either John's or my Spanish.

San Cristóbal was an interesting, but sleepy little town with a lot of Indians, as well as Mexicans and Guatemalans. Chiapas later become known for being the center for several insurrections that were a threat to the government. There weren't many tourists there but Dave and I browsed around town with no problem while John was in his meetings. I know a bit of Spanish from studying it for my Ph.D. language requirement and my trips to Puerto Rico. After a few days, we flew from San Cristóbal to Acapulco for a couple days of relaxation. On the way, we saw some ancient ruins around Oaxaca, I believe. We circled it for a good look but did not land. We had a fine time in Acapulco seeing the local sights. We took a boat tour around the harbor, including a visit to the famous divers that dive from great heights from a cliff into the ocean.

A couple days later, we flew to Mexico City to do some sightseeing and shopping. On the way to Mexico City, we had to fly over the surrounding mountains that were about 14,000 feet high. We were flying visual and had no oxygen so flying over 14,000 feet high gets to where the oxygen is a little thin. John skirted the highest peaks and we had no problems; the scenery was great. The next day we wanted to see the pyramids, and I think John and Dave did, but I spent the day in bed at our hotel. Montezuma's Revenge really got me, until someone brought me some medicine for it. A day or two later we flew back to Dallas with no difficulty. This whole trip was memorable because it was the first and only time that the three of us ever got away together as adults for a relaxing event. Because Dave died about 10 years ago, we can never do it again.

*Stanford Executive Program.* In Spring 1975, Mr. Hekman asked me if I would be interested in taking some time off for a refresher course in executive management. There is one nearby, at Airlie House in Warenton, Virginia[1] that caters mostly to government people that I suggested. But, Hekman preferred that I go to one of the graduate schools of business at one of the major universities. He said I could pick whichever school appealed to me. I considered mainly two schools, the one at the Harvard Graduate School of Business and the one at Stanford Graduate School of Business (the *"Harvard of the West"*). They were both

---
1 http://www.airlie.com.

very expensive, something like $6,000 for a 6-week program, which seemed like a lot to me.[2] Hekman told me to go to the best one and I chose the Stanford Executive Program at Stanford in Palo Alto, California. They had a lot of big name professors in the program. It would also give me a chance to renew my association with California that appealed to me since I am a Berkeley graduate but have lived in the East since receiving my Ph.D.

I went to Stanford that summer and had a grand time. I was surprised at how much the program repeated the material I had covered at Berkeley 15 years earlier, even though I was not in the School of Business at Berkeley, but it was a good refresher. We had first-rate professors from the regular Graduate School of Business at Stanford, such as Professor Harold Leavitt who taught organizational behavior and human resource management, and Professor Charles Horngren who taught accounting. Alan Enthoven, former Secretary of Defense, was also on the faculty. He was well-known for his macro-economic simulations, used by the Federal Reserve under Alan Greenspan, which was something new to the program.

I particularly enjoyed meeting and interacting with a lot of industry executives from all over the world. There were only eight of us from government, out of about 105 students in to-

---
2 In 2008 the cost was $52,000.

tal; about one-fourth were from outside the U.S. There was one person in the program that I had known at Iowa State as an undergraduate; he was an executive with Monsanto in St. Louis at the time. A couple other students that I became acquainted with were Bill Linscott, a personnel director from Boeing Aircraft in Seattle, and Chris Walliker from Astonia Holdings Ltd in England. I took a set of tennis lessons, which was a new sport for me, and also enjoyed playing the golf course at Stanford during my spare time. It is a very challenging course and I found time to play several times during the 6-week period, often with my old friend Chuck Enrst. He had retired from FNS as the western region's regional administrator, who I had worked with in San Francisco for several years. He had always lived in Palo Alto and commuted to San Francisco when working for FNS. I could see why he enjoyed living there.

*Family Trip*. In July-August 1977, I was asked to go to San Francisco to meet with A.T. Kearney regarding a study of the Food Commodity Program they were doing for FNS. I also wanted to go to Houston to attend the annual meetings of the American School Food Service Association, so we decided to take a memorable family auto trip across country to visit both locations on the same trip. My wife and I took our two youngest kids, John and Karen, who were ages 14 and 16 at the time, so they could see the countryside. We saw 8,400 miles of it. It was to be the last long auto trip we ever took together as a family, so it was good we decided to do it then. It was also a celebration of our 25th wedding anniversary. We came back through Oskaloosa, Iowa to see my parents and many of our relatives at a big celebration at Central Reformed Church where we were married. I bought my wife some beautiful Indian jewelry (a "squash blossom" necklace made of silver, turquoise and coral in Phoenix) to celebrate the occasion. We also visited the south ridge of the Grand Canyon after leaving Phoenix and taking an indirect route to San Francisco. It took us an entire month, starting on July 24, even though we made good use of our time. Every day was carefully planned.

*Memorable Speeches.* I gave lots of speeches while working for the Food and Nutrition Service, often filling in for Mr. Hekman when he was unavailable or on a subject on which he knew I was most familiar. Two that stand out in my mind included one at the University of Georgia in Athens where I filled-in for Secretary of Agriculture Bob Bergland who had to cancel on short notice. We had a large snow storm at that time and he may have been snowed in somewhere. The administrator of the Economics, Statistics and Cooperatives Service[3], Ken Farrell, had

---

3 Also known by the name, Economic Research Service.

asked me to do it because the subject was one with which I was familiar. But, I am still sure the audience was disappointed in not seeing the Secretary of Agriculture.

Another speech was a presentation in March 1980 at the Plaza Hotel across the street from Central Park in New York City where I stayed. I was quite impressed with the hotel. I was there to address the prestigious National Conference Board on the topic of impacts of industry concentration in the food industry. I had researched this topic thoroughly as a graduate student at Berkeley and kept up with the subject over the years.

## Mr. Hekman's Retirement

Mr. Hekman resigned soon after Jimmy Carter was elected President in November 1976, at about age 63. As FNS Administrator, Hekman had had a politically-appointed, Schedule C position, so he served at the discretion of the president and secretary of agriculture.

At his retirement, Mr. Hekman gave me a copy of his picture with the following note:

> *Dear Steve:*
>
> *Thanks for all you've done for FNS and for the Department of Agriculture. Your role has not been easy, but the accomplishments are very real. I'm sure the evaluations and studies you have initiated will provide the data needed for right decisions toward program effectiveness. I've appreciated you friendship.*
>
> *Ed Hekman 11/22/76*

Ed had a house being built at Hilton Head, South Carolina, where he and his wife had vacationed frequently. He was an avid tennis player and he was looking forward to playing a lot of tennis there. He actually moved down there prior to the new house being completed. Soon thereafter, while playing doubles with his wife he went back for a lob and lost his balance. He hit his head on the court that gave him a concussion. He died the next day. Ironically, the day he died I was scheduled to have lunch in Washington with him and Mary Jane Fiske. He told us he wanted to discuss his future plans. I never knew just what he had in mind but I suspected he wanted to come back to Washington at the end of Carter's term if the Republicans regained the White House. Mary Jane had been his legislative assistant in FNS prior to his retirement.

### New Administrator

With the Democrats now in office, FNS took a new policy direction. Our new assistant secretary in charge of food programs was Carol Forman, a former consumer advocate who often sparred vociferously with Mr. Hekman on food program policy issues. She appointed Lewis Strauss and later Robert (Bob) Greenspan as the new FNS Administrators. Greenspan, in particular, was another vocal former consumer advocate.

As a career civil servant, I continued to do my job. My job as assistant to the administrator was taken away but I remained as head of the Program Evaluation and Economic Analysis Staff. I was not as busy as previously, but I still had plenty to do. Obviously, I was on top of a lot of information and managed various studies that the new administration needed. Also, the budget for the current year could not be changed. But, my job was not as much fun, so I began looking for another job.

On March 3, Strauss asked me to attend a staff meeting held by Secretary of Agriculture Bergland. The subject was the current economic situation facing agriculture, presented by Howard Hjort, so being an agricultural economist, I was asked to attend. Jim Webster, Director of the Office of Governmental and Public Affairs also gave a presentation on the Grain Reserve Program. Neither Strauss nor Carol Forman would have understood either subject.

In early 1978, I presented a major paper at a food policy seminar sponsored by ERS, USDA entitled, *"Evaluation of the Effectiveness and Efficiency in Food Programs."* It was one of five related seminars coordinated by my friend Bill (William) Boehm that were all published in a composite report, entitled Agricultural Food Policy Review (Hiemstra, 1978a). They were intended to focus on the interrelatedness of food and agricultural policy.

In June 1978, I was asked to be a member of the President's Reorganization Task Force. This Task Force included Charlie French, Chair of the Task Force, and Allan Johnson, both of whom were agricultural economists no longer in USDA and both of whom I had been closely associated with for many years. I believe Allan was Domestic Advisor to the President located in the Executive Office of the President, and Charlie was also in the Executive Office. They were concerned with reorganization of various programs among departments, but neither one knew much about the food programs. For example, they were considering moving the child nutrition programs from USDA to a new education department, mainly because these programs are managed at the state level by state education departments. That was not a good idea in my opinion; they are food programs not education programs. Even so, Assistant Secretary Foreman recommended the move to the Congress. The Congress agreed to set up the new department but did not concur with the moving the child nutrition programs to the new department.

Another suggested change related to cashing out the FSP in favor of an expanded welfare reform program which I did not support, as I have discussed previously. I was asked to develop a paper discussing both of these suggestions and possible alternative options. After the task force was terminated, I was giving an award in the name of the President, which I thought looked impressive, but it did not carry a cash award. I was just pleased to be consulted on both of these policy issues, particularly by a democratic administration.

# COUNCIL ON WAGE AND PRICE STABILITY

The FAT Division

Industry Meetings

Second and Third Years

Program Evaluation

Other Travel

On October 24, 1978, the Jimmy Carter Administration announced the formation of a new organization within the Executive Office of the President called the Council on Wage and Price Stability (CWPS).[1] The CPI had been climbing rapidly since the 1974-75 recession and was considered to be out of control. By 1978, prices were increasing at an annual rate of 9 percent per annum, which was unacceptable high. The overall objective of CWPS was to reverse this rapid increase in prices.

About two days after the announcement of the formation of CPWS, I received a phone call from Dawson Ahalt, Chairman of the World Food and Agricultural Outlook and Situation Board, asking if I would be available to take a temporary position with CPWS to represent USDA's interest in food prices. I knew Dawson well since we had worked in the same division for several years and I had told him that I was looking for a new position. He knew of my earlier work with ERS in forecasting retail food prices and in conducting studies analyzing the demand for food, which gave me a good background for the job. I agreed rather

---

[1] The Council on Wage and Price Stability was established within the Executive Office of the President by Act of August 24, 1974 (88 Stat. 750; 12 U.S.C. 19011 note), as amended. In addition, by Executive Order No. 12092 (November 1, 1978), and Executive Order 12161 (44 FR 56663), the President authorized the Council to develop standards implementing the voluntary program of wage and price restraint which the President initiated.

quickly to give the job careful consideration.

In a day or two I had the job and was asked to report for duty immediately. The first assignment was to be one of about 20 people in the New Executive Office Building who were fielding phone calls from people calling the White House asking for details of the new program. We were given a white paper that explained the program in general but there were many unanswered questions; it was really a work in process. After reading this paper, I was put into a large room in the New Executive Office Building with the others answering questions from the general public about the details of this new wage and price program that the President had announced. Following was a hectic couple weeks during which we helped develop the details of the program on the fly working closely with Barry Bosworth who had been given the position as director of the program. He reported to Alfred Kahn, Assistant to the President. Bosworth was a well-known economist from the Brookings Institute and Kahn was the well-known economist from Cornell University who gained fame as the author and promoter of deregulation of the airline industry which had occurred just a few years earlier.

The price standard was defined as limiting the allowable average rate of price increases allowed for individual companies to one-half percentage point less than that company's prices had increased during the base period of the last quarter of 1977 in relation to the last quarter of 1978. Obviously, price increases could not be controlled unless wages were also controlled since they account for the largest share of costs for most companies. The pay standard was defined simply as a limitation on the average rate of hourly compensation (including fringe benefits) to 7 percent (annual rate) over the base quarter of July-September 1978. Based on averages, both of these standards were designed to avoid impeding productivity increases (CWPS, 1979b).

I pointed out immediately that the price standard being based only on selling prices would not be reasonable with respect to either the retailing or wholesaling industries unless somehow the cost of goods sold were also held to similar standards. Bosworth and Kahn agreed, so we developed a percentage-gross-margin standard for retail and wholesale companies, and a dollar gross margin standard for food processing and manufacturing companies. Petroleum refiners were also allowed to use the dollar gross margin standard.

The allowable percentage gross margin for retailers and wholesalers was to increase only in line with any margin trend that occurred over a three-year base period. Dollar gross margins for food manufacturers and refiners in total were limited to 6 percent from the base quarter of July-September 1978 to the fourth quarter of the program year. In addition, there was to be an allowance for increases in volume. The dollar gross margin was more stringent since it allowed only a dollar-for-dollar pass through of price increases while the percentage gross margin allowed a pass through of percentage increases in purchased goods (CWPS, 1979b).

If a firm had uncontrollable prices and could not meet the price or margin standards, then it was allowed to be judged by the profit standard. This standard required that net operating profits as a percentage of sales stay below the average of the best two out of the last three years.

## The FAT Division

Soon thereafter, Barry Bosworth asked me take the job of overseeing the program related to the bulk of all wholesale and retail trade, including food away from home, plus food, beverage, textiles, apparel, leather, and tobacco processing and manufacturing (SEC codes 20-23 and 50-59,) industries.

These industries accounted for more than one-third of all companies (based on compliance reports) monitored by the Council. I was initially given a small division with six or eight economist positions, plus a secretary and file clerk, which was later expanded to 12 positions.

I gave the tiny new division the title of the Food, Agriculture, and Trade Division (FAT), with the humorous acronym of the FAT Division. We used the title of division chief rather than division director used at USDA. I was to be paid by CWPS but officially on loan from USDA and I could return there upon termination of the Council. I hired Gar Forsht and Rich Platt, economists from my old outfit in FNS, USDA, and Terry Crawford, an economist from ERS, USDA, who I had worked with earlier.

Ours was one of five divisions in CWPS in the Office of Price Monitoring (OPM) headed first by Jack Triplet who was on loan from Bureau of Labor Statistics where he was a Deputy

Commissioner and after the first year, Robert Baesemann. OPM was focused on the price and margin standards. Our Office was in charge of operational management of all of the price and margin standards but had no responsibility for the pay standards. Triplett/Baesemann reported to Barry Bosworth who took a personal interest in all of the program's policies and procedures.

In October 1978, Barry took several of us to a major meeting of CEOs and their general counsels held in Los Angeles, California to explain the program to all of the large companies on the West Coast. The large hotel conference room was crowded and I was impressed with the attention that Barry received from the group.

The standards were voluntary and applied only to companies with $250 million or more in annual sales. But, it included 447 out of the Fortune 500 industrial companies in the first year of the program. They were each identified by name in a press release (CWPS, 1979a). About 95 percent of the targeted companies provided the data requested by the Council during the first year.

However, in March 1980, the threshold for the second year of the program was lowered to companies with sales exceeding $100 million. But, the rate of response to data requests dropped sharply during the second year. It was estimated that these companies accounted for about 30 percent of the nation's total number of transactions during the period of the program.

Individual farmers were not subject to the standards because of their small size. Also, producers of primary agricultural products and commodities traded on open market exchanges were exempt from the standards. However, some large corporate firms would be large enough and some of their collective organizations such as the farmer owned cooperatives, like Sunkist Oranges in California, were subject to it. The Council was also concerned with national policies such as USDA price support programs on dairy products and sugar, tariffs on agricultural products, and related activities that have overall impacts on farm and food prices. I gave a presentation to the National Association of State Departments of Agriculture in February 1979 in Washington D.C. to discuss these issues (Hiemstra, 1979c). James Graham, President of the NASDA organization and Commissioner of Agriculture from North Carolina, presided at the meeting.

I coordinated closely with USDA. Dawson Ahalt was designated as USDA's designated liaison with the Council, but I heard directly from Howard Hjort, Chief Economist of USDA, on important issues. For example, Howard wrote us a long memo after the end of the first year complaining that the gross margin standard was not strict enough. I sent them regular reports of our activities. McFall Lamb in ERS[1] sent me monthly reports on food and agriculture price trends and price spreads. We incorporated this information into our *"Monthly Food Price Review"* which was released publicly by my division as attachments to CWPS press releases, March 1979-March 1980. The reports were continued through December 1980 for internal use (CWPS, 1979-1980).

The first reporting requirement of the program was due on February 15, 1979, when the target companies had to tell the Council the composition of their company in terms of 4-digit Standard Industrial Code (SIC) categories of business. They had to explain how they intended to operate under the program, that is, which standard they wanted to operate under. They also had to provide the baseline data relevant to the selected standard. Quarterly data then had to be provided during the course of the program giving average prices and/or margins to demonstrate compliance.

The AFL-CIA was not too happy with our wage standard, as you might expect. In fact, President George Meany took the

---

[1] ERS was actually called Economics, Statistics, and Cooperative Service at the time.

Council to court trying to get it ruled unconstitutional. They won their initial suit, but it was overturned upon appeal. In early 1980, the 7-percent wage limitation was relaxed to a range of 7 1/2 to 9 annual percent which was still considered too low in view of price inflation as measured by the CPI of 13 percent (annual rate) in the last half of 1979 (CWPS, 1981). The CPI actually peaked at 18.1 percent (annual rate) in the first quarter of 1980.

The Council was sensitive to the wage standard being too restrictive because of the possibility of causing labor shortages. As a result, collective bargaining wages were allowed under the program as long as the labor agreements allowed for demonstrable increases in labor productivity. But, non-union wages without formal cost-of-living adjustments were still expected to abide by the standards and they likely resulted in lower costs of production in those industries. Non-union employees still constitute the majority of the work force in the country.

All of the industries took the standards quite seriously, even though they were voluntary, and they usually filed the necessary quarterly reporting forms that we needed to monitor their compliance. We held the companies accountable with a finding of noncompliance with the standards if they ignored us. Such findings were published as general press releases which we drafted and sent to them for information before publication. If the company involved had problems meeting the price standards, they could apply for an exception based on the rate of profits they were earning.

To get such an exception, they had to justify their requests by showing us their books. This usually entailed their coming to Washington with detailed accounts of their costs and profits earned. Many major companies came in to see us, including several of the major food chains and beer manufacturing companies. Most of them did a good job in justifying their requests, but a surprising number of these large companies apparently did not keep good accounting records.

One major catalog retailer's response demonstrated a good example of the program's impacts. I drafted a notice of noncompliance for this company when their data indicated excessive prices were being charged. The draft notice, which went to them over Bosworth's signature, gave them just a few days to come into compliance to avoid publication of the notice. They called back immediately and asked for a meeting to discuss the problem. Their CEO along with their General Counsel personally showed up for the meeting in Bosworth 's office with me and our General Counsel, Sally Katzen. To avoid our publication of their noncompliance with the standards, they agreed to lower their upcoming summer catalog prices by 5 percent across the board. That was one of the clear-cut success stories that we could demonstrate.

In total, the FAT Division issued 53 notices of probable noncompliance over the two year period of the Council, 46 of them during the first year. Almost all of them were resolved favorably to the companies involved after promising specific corrective action. Some $57 million worth of corrective action was specifically identified. Eleven companies were formally declared out of compliance by December 15, 1980.

## Industry Meetings

We held industry meetings with a large number of industry association groups and responded to many requests for personal presentations of various industry groups. Two industry meetings related to my division in particular, the retail food industry and the wholesale food industry. They focused specifically on the subject of how to define gross margins. That definition got tricky for retailers that manufacture many of their own store-branded products and consequently do not have arms-length determined, supply prices.

I met several times with Kent Christensen, Senior Vice President with the Food Marketing Institute, on this and related issues; he and I were longstanding friends. In the second year of the program, we largely solved the problem by requiring retail and wholesale companies to report manufacturing operations of $50 million or more as separate entities under the price standard rather than lumped under the gross margin standard. George Koch, CEO of Grocery Manufacturers of America (GMA), was quite unhappy with this requirement of dividing their operations.

GMA was one of the industry groups with which I had maintained a close relationship. George Koch, came in to see me about every month or he would invite me for lunch at the Four Seasons, his regular lunch spot. I also met regularly with their technical people who stayed in touch with their food manufacturing members. I met with them formally in November 1978 when the program was in its infant stage, and in June 1979, GMA invited me to the Greenbrier Hotel at White Sulpher Springs, West Virginia to update their members on our program at their annual meeting, which was a big fancy affair (Hiemstra, 1978b and 1979e).

I addressed the foodservice distributors in September 1979 at their annual conference held at the Hyatt Regency Hotel in Washington DC (Hiemstra, 1979g). I followed a famous person named Howard Ruff on the program, and was followed by Senator Max Baucus from Montana, who was asked specifically to react to my presentation.

The Milk Industry Foundation was another industry group that stayed in close contact with my Division (Hiemstra, 1978b). The milk industry is one of the most important recipients of USDA price support activities. I met also with the American Meat Industry which had set up a special task force to relate to the wage and price standards but that industry is very competitive and had little to fear from our program (Hiemstra, 1979a).

The Southeastern Food Canners and Freezers Association invited me to Ashville, North Carolina to address their Association's annual meeting to explain the price standards (Hiemstra, 1979h). I gave their keynote address, and still remember the lovely view of the mountains from their hotel. My wife went with me on this trip, and after the meeting we toured the Vanderbilt mansion which was nearby. It is a beautiful place.

In March 1979, I was invited by Congressman Ted Weiss to address the 20th District Community Conference on the subject of *Inflation, the Economy and You* (Hiemstra, 1979c). The meeting was held at Riverside Church, NYC. The subject was whether the program should be voluntary or mandatory as the price control program had been in the early 1970s. I argued that the current voluntary program was much better because mandatory programs could lead to black market pricing without strong measure to police prices, as well as its questionable constitutionality for a democracy. The earlier program had not been considered very successful.

I was scheduled to give a presentation about our program to the Executive Committee of the National Associations of Tobacco Distributors, meeting in at Sea Pines, Hilton Head, South

Carolina. It was a high priority request by way of the White House. But, at the last minute, it was cancelled because of a hurricane scare. It was too bad that it was cancelled, because I was to be on a program with Congressman Jack Kemp and at a great location. I had been asked to address the importance of energy relative to inflation. I did learn, in preparation for the meeting, that energy made up 4.1 percent of costs for food processors, but only 1.3 percent for tobacco manufacturing. But, it had a weight 8.5 of percent in the CPI.

I worked closely with Alfred Kahn's office in setting up a group meeting of 50 leaders from the food processing and manufacturing industries with Jimmy Carter in the Roosevelt Room of the White House on June 3, 1979. He and Kahn were concerned with the rapid increases in food prices that were occurring. I attended the meeting but the meeting was hosted by Alfred Kahn. I also set up a smaller meeting with Alfred Kahn in his office in the Old Executive Office Building[1] on December 5, 1979, with 11 leaders of the alcoholic and non-alcoholic beverage industries. Mixing these two groups together was not a good idea because of their different types of problems.

I have a copy of an interesting handwritten note dated

---

[1] The Old Executive Office Building is next to the White House on 17th Street.

August 17, 1979 on White House letterhead and addressed to Bob Bergland[2] and Fred Kahn, and signed by J.C.[3]:

> "Do not drop the food price/profit issue. Both of you continue to hit it hard and publicly. Retail prices are excessively high. Assume our data are accurate until proven otherwise. Fritz[4] will help."

---

2 Secretary of Agriculture
3 Presumably, Jimmy Carter
4 Senator from Minnesota.

## Second and Third Years

The second year of the programs allowed for some changes that became obviously needed during the first year's operation. In particular, more precision was provided in definitions of industries and their specific requirements were clarified (CWPS, 1980). For example, the companies eligible for the percentage gross margin standard were defined to exclude their manufacturing and processing operations that exceeded $50 million. The price and wage standards were increased to allow in part for the increase in prices that occurred during the first year, as noted above.

We had a longstanding complaint from the broiler industry, mainly the National Broiler Council, asking that their industry be exempt from the standards because there was no national market for their products and theirs was a very competitive industry. The Council, supported by USDA, disagreed that the broiler industry met the criteria for exemption because of their large-sized companies and relatively concentrated industry that contrasted directly with their small buyers and suppliers. Finally, after we held many meetings with representatives from USDA and others on the Council, on November 5, 1980, Council Director Bob Russell met with representatives from broiler industry and concurred that the Council would exempt them from the standards. By then, the program was winding down so the decision was largely academic.

The third year's program regulations were published in the Federal Register on November 20, 1980, but were never put into effect in view of the election of Ronald Reagan for president and his avowed intention to discontinue the program. On December 20, Charles Schultz replaced Alfred Kahn as caretaker Chairman of the Council; R. Robert Russell had earlier replaced Barry Bosworth as the Director. He had been Bosworth's Deputy Director. Companies were informed to continue to abide by the standards but asked to not submit reports in view of it likely termination.

## *Program Evaluation*

Over the two years of the price standards, retail food prices increased 21 percent (September 1980 vs. September 1978), which was a huge increase. But, nonfood retail prices increased even more, 27 percent, during this period, and the CPI all items increased 26 percent. Wholesale food prices increased 18 percent. At the same time, the food marketing cost index increased by 26 percent; labor costs alone were up 20 percent. These figures suggest that our program had some aggregate positive impacts in restraining price increases even though inflation was still alive and well.

In January 1981, my division prepared a 100-page unpublished report which contains the above data plus a detailed analysis of many aspects of the two-year program operated by the FAT Division, but it contains no confidential individual company information (COWPS, 1981a). This report should be invaluable if a new wage and price standards program were ever to be reinstituted.

I gave several presentations to professional groups assessing the standards of our program from various perspectives as the program progressed:

1. I discussed our plans for monitoring the pay and price program with the National Economists Club at their meeting in May 1979 at the Black Horse Tavern in Washington DC (Hiemstra 1979d).

2. In November 1979, I gave a paper on the *"Impacts of the Pay and Price Standards on the Food Industry,"* at the Southern Economic Association at their annual meetings in Atlanta (Hiemstra, 1979i). It included results of a statistical model developed by Rich Platt and I that showed that retail food prices in 1979 were below the level that they would have been expected to be in the absence of the food price program. A paper distributed at the meeting by the Federal Reserve Bank of New York, by Bennett and Greene came to the same conclusion. The session was sponsored by the Society of Government Economists and chaired by Joyce Zickler from the Board of Governors of the Federal Reserve.

3. In March 1980, I was invited by The Conference Board to give a presentation on the structural implications of the price and wage programs on antitrust issues (Hiemstra, 1980a). It was held at the Plaza Hotel across the street from Central Park in New York City. It was an impressive group.

4. Also in March, 1980, I made a presentation at the Washington Farm Convention on the impacts of the program on agriculture, sponsored by Congressmen Tom Harkins, Tom Bedell, and Berkley Dashall, at the Cannon House Office Building in Washington

DC (Hiemstra, 1980b).

5. I discussed *"Effectiveness of the Voluntary Standard Price Standards and Their Future Role"* at the School of Business, University of Texas at Arlington in April 1980 (Hiemstra, l 980c). I also addressed the historical perspective of our program at the awards ceremony of the Omicron Delta Epsilon Economics Fraternity of the School of Business the same day. Professor Tansey sent me an unusually warm letter of appreciation after I returned home. He had heard me speak at the Southern Economic Association meetings in Atlanta which led to my invitation.

6. In October, 1980, I gave a presentation related to *"Standards, Procedures and Impacts"* to Cornell University's Agricultural Economics Department at Ithaca, New York (Hiemstra, 1980d).

By then, Rich Platt and I had seven quarters of measurable data with the program and had developed some statistical demand models to verify the measurable impacts of the program on food prices. By adding a shift variable to a standard aggregate food demand model since 1972, we measured the impacts of the price standards. It showed that retail food prices were 2.3 percent lower during the seven quarters of experience with the price standards compared with the 27 periods prior to implementing the standards.

Despite the above presentations, a lot of concerns continued to be raised as to whether or not the Council's program did any good in holding down prices, particularly after the program had been in effect for two years. Raw material price increases were impossible to control, and wage standards were largely ignored in many industries. These were not problems with the gross margin standards because costs were passed through to consumers, but that was not the case with the price standard. Actually, the price standard was in place for companies in only about one-third of the industry. The gross margin standards accounted for another third and the profit exception covered the remaining third.

An econometric evaluation of all industries in the program conducted in January 1981, just before the termination of the program, concluded that labor cost increases were reduced by about one percentage point as a result of the wage standard during the first year of the program (CWPS, 1981b). Since allowable wages were increased by about 2 percent annually during the second year, the impacts of the program during the second year likely had less effect. The same study concluded that the price standard likely resulted in about one-half of one percent decline in prices. This small impact was judged to not be statistically significant.

A survey was conducted of a sample of company participants near the end of the program. The 2,856 companies reported estimated average costs of administering the program over the two years at $108,000. While many companies regarded this cost as a real burden, others indicated that it helped them improve their own administrative procedures.

Personally, my work with the CWPS turned out to be an enjoyable job in which I learned a tremendous amount about the workings of both the food industry and the higher levels of Government. When the Reagan administration came into office in January 1981, the Council was dismantled as one of Reagan's first actions. I stayed until the end and was at the Council for two years and two months. Those of us from USDA returned to our previous jobs with no problem.

There were two occasions that provided some personal benefits in working for the White House. The first occasion was when we were invited to the White House on the 4th of July to view the evening fireworks from the lawn of the White House (I think during both years we were there). Our daughter, Karen, was particularly impressed with shaking hands with President Carter. I think she went through the line three or four times.

The second occasion was in the closing weeks of the Council's life, as well as that of President Carter's presidency, he invited all members of the Executive Office to come by the Oval Office and have their picture taken individually with the President. I thought that was a nice parting gesture and I still have the picture 27 years later. There were some 230 employees of CWPS at its peak.

I always thought it was amusing to have a position in the White House under Jimmy Carter because I am a registered republican and never voted for Carter. But, since I was a career economist, that is the way the civil service is supposed to work and no one ever questioned by motives or professionalism.

## *Other Travel*

*I* was able to keep up with many of my USDA and other professional obligations during the time I was at CWPS. For example, in October 1978, I addressed the Kansas State School Food Service Association in Wichita. In November 1978, I went to Kansas again to give a graduate seminar jointly to the Dietetics, Restaurant, and Institutional Management Department and the Department of Agricultural Economics at Kansas State University on the subject of research needs in evaluation of food assistance programs.

I went to Chicago the same month and again in March 1979 to Purdue University in Indiana to consult with other editors of a book entitled, *Future Frontiers in Agricultural Marketing Research*, for which I prepared a chapter (Hiemstra, 1983c).

In May 1979, I attended the Eastern Economic Association Meetings in Boston and introduced Assistant Secretary Carol Forman who spoke on evaluation of the food programs.

In September 1979, I went to Boston again and met with a long-time friend of mine in the Graduate School of Business, Harvard University when some of his students presented a case study related to the FSP. He had contacted me months earlier for some background information for the case.

*Germany*. In July 1979, my wife and I went to Göttingen, Germany, to visit our son Stephen who had studied at the University of Göttingen for a year, and to bring him back home. While there, I also gave a presentation at the Agricultural Economics Department at the university related to the U.S. wage and price programs (Hiemstra, 1979). Then, we toured Europe together for about three weeks and had a fine time. This was a time of rapidly increasing gasoline prices so we bought a new, bright yellow, diesel Volkswagen Rabbit and brought it back to the U.S. at the end of our tour. At that time, VW's were expensive and hard to even buy in the U.S. because of their popularity for gas efficiency. We got about 50 miles per gallon of diesel, and drove it over 100,000 miles over the next decade, and then gave it away.

On our tour, we drove first north and west into Belgium, seeing the ancient town of Bruegge which was very impressive. Then, we drove into the Netherlands and marveled at the fabulous dikes and darns along the way that have been built to control the water after their historic flood in 1953. We visited Amsterdam and saw the Van Gogh[1] and Rijks[2] museums, which I had seen and enjoyed on my first trip to the Netherlands a de-

---

1 http://www.VanGoghMuseum.nl
2 www.RijksMuseum.nl

cade earlier. Then, we drove to Eta in the southeastern part of the country where my mother's family originated and where the Tysseling Mill is located. The Tysseling Mill, built well before the 1600's, is now a historical monument.

One of the Tyselling family members had carved his initials and the date (about 1661) on one of the beams holding up the mill. Finally, we visited Friesland where my father's family originated near Dokkum.

From there we drove into Germany and visited the family of Stephen's friend who lived on a dairy farm there. He actually worked on the irrigation system there. We drove through the East Germany corridor to reach Berlin, which was very historic to see. The border with East Germany was rather frightening to look across. From there, we drove south to Munich, which has a very impressive castle and other fascinating things. We had a good local guide who was a friend of our son. We also toured a Nazi concentration camp on the outskirts of Munich that was nauseating. It still had the ovens in which they burned bodies of the Jews and other political prisoners. We then briefly visited Vienna, Austria, where we saw an ancient castle on a hill, and then drove to Burchesgarden, Hitler's favorite hideout in the beautiful mountains of southern Germany. We drove north and west through the Black Forest, Innsbruck, Switzerland, and a corner of France. We also saw some memorable memorials to the Battle of the Bulge, and went on to Luxemburg where we shipped our VW to the U.S. and flew home.

I was President of the Society of Government Economists (SGE) in 1979. I chaired the annual business meeting on March 14. The monthly meetings consisted of presentations by local economic professionals of general interest, which I selected and invited to the meetings. One person of interest who spoke to the Society while I was president was director of the Congressional Budget Office. She later became deputy director of the Federal Reserve to Greenspan.

Another job of mine as president of SGE was to organize two or three sessions of annual meetings to be presented at the annual meetings of the ASSA which meet normally between Christmas and New Year's Day at New York, Chicago, San Francisco, or Washington DC. The AEA and the American Finance Association (AFA) were the main focus of the meetings, but the AAEA is a member as well at least during the winter meetings.

ASSA draws several thousand economists to their meetings each year. I tried to attend many of them and often gave papers sponsored by SGE or AEA. I last attended these meetings in December 2004 held at the convention center in Washington DC.

Other trips I took during this time period included attendance at the annual meetings of AAEA in Champaign IL during July 1980. In November, I attended some meetings at Airlie House in Warrenton, Virginia[3], which were focused on the economics of advertising.

---

3 http://www.Airlie.com.

# RETURN TO THE FOOD NUTRITION SERVICE, USDA

Changing of the Guard

Other Travel

## *Changing of the Guard*

With the election of Ronald Reagan as President and the demise of the CWPS, I returned to the FNS, USDA in January 1981, along with Gar Forsht and Rich Platt. By then, Carol Forman was gone from her job as Assistant Secretary of Agriculture in charge of the food programs, and Bob Greenspan was out as Administrator of FNS[1]. In his place, G. William (Bill) Hoagland was hired from a staff position on the Senate Budget Committee to be the new Administrator of FNS. Bill Hoagland had worked for me before getting his job with the Senate. I hired him right out of graduate school at Pennsylvania State University where he worked on a study of the FSP under contract to FNS by Pat Madden, so he knew the food programs well.

I was now given the position as Director of the Economic Analysis Staff in the Office of Policy, Planning and Evaluation (OPPE), at the same GS-15 level that I had when I was at CWPS and earlier at FNS (now at Step 8). This Office had been created by the previous administration to do program evaluation and policy analysis. Bill Hoagland hired Barry White as the new Director of OPPE. I was disappointed at not getting the job since I had had responsibility for the same duties under Hekman, in

---

1 Both of them to this day are still working as consumer advocates.

the previous republican administration. But, OPPE was by then a much larger organization than I had had. I was still given many of the same kinds of work I had done earlier but it was more focused on economic analysis than program evaluation.

Barry White assigned program evaluation to an evaluation staff under Mike Wargo who had been doing some large program evaluation studies, largely under contract, while I was at CWPS. White had been hired from outside of USDA and he did not last long in his position; by December he was gone and his job was taken temporarily by George Braley.

In May, 1981, Gar Forsht and I conducted a study, *"Impact of Indexation on the Food Stamp Program."* The article was never published but its findings would likely have proven to be rather controversial. Between fiscal years 1970 and 1980, per capita food stamp benefits were found to have increased by 49 percent in real terms, from $9.44 to $14.03 per month. That is, after dividing current data by the CPI price index for food at home. That is a substantial increase that drove the budget up considerably.

Two-thirds of that increase was due to increases in deductions from incomes claimed by recipient households which were put on an escalator basis after the elimination of the EPR. A second reason for the increase was due to applying price escalators to the cost of the Thrifty Food Plan in total rather than applying it only to the value of the bonus stamps provided to recipients. Average monthly real incomes of recipients had increased only 6 percent during this period but deductions had increased by $56 per month per household. As a result, benefits per person had increased at a much higher rate (12.9 percent) than either the CPI, food at home index (8.3 percent) or the Thrifty Food Plan which is used to adjust the allotment levels.

On July 13, 1981, I was interviewed on Channel 22, Maryland Public Broadcasting, on the subject of the impacts of the FSP on U.S. agriculture.

In October 1981, I was invited to present a paper at a national conference held at the University of Maryland, called *"Perspectives on Food and Agricultural Policy Research Workshop."* I presented a paper, *"Researching Domestic Food Assistance Programs,"* which discussed the difference among program evaluation, program analysis, and policy analysis. Often those terms are used almost interchangeably but they are quite different. I also outlined FNS plans for program evaluations. The workshop was sponsored jointly by the Farm Foundation and ERS, USDA and attended by a large number of respected agricultural policy analysts. Bill Hoagland was invited to attend but he asked me to cover for him. The workshop published the proceedings of the conference (Hiemstra 1981b).

In March 1982, the Economic Analysis Staff, including myself, was transferred to the office of the Deputy Administrator for Financial Management, Ray Pugh, from the Office of Analysis and Evaluation (which had been renamed from OPPE). My staff was renamed the Management Information Division to reflect my increased focus on data collection and analysis in supporting the budget, as well as conducting program projections for other purposes. In my files, I found a set of 5-year projections of food stamp participation and costs that were sent to the General Accounting Office in April 1982. I should check to see how these projections compared with actual data.

By that time, we had a new administrator, Bob Laird. Bill Hoagland had returned to the Senate Budget Office where he worked for the majority leader and has been there ever since. Bill got blamed for the controversy over declaring ketchup a vegetable for purposes of the SLP. He did not deserve the negative publicity involved. Up until that time, there had been increasing interest in the school lunch program to change the "Type A" meal requirement to allow for all of the nutrients being served in the program rather than only the specified food components of the meal, as outlined earlier. This change later became known as nutrient standards, which were finalized a decade or so later. But, at the time Bill Hoagland was administrator, the consumer advocates looked for any reason to criticize FNS circulated information. What was happening was that the nutrients in ketchup as well as the nutrients in all other items served in the lunch were counted toward the meal pattern in the pilot nutrient standard being pilot tested. It is hard to believe, but that criticism became so widespread that Bill stepped down from his position and left the agency.

In my new focus as director of the Management Information Division, we developed a set of tables providing detailed program data related to participation and costs of all FNS programs that we sent to the administrator and all FNS offices that requested them. It was a comprehensive set of 30 tables that were printed monthly showing cumulative totals within fiscal years and comparisons with the same month a year earlier. I also used these data as the basis for a monthly report and personal presentation to the administrator and his immediate staff. It included a set of colored charts that highlighted trends and points of policy interest. At that time, colored charts were not in general use and quite expensive. We could not then afford a colored Xerox machine. But after searching, we found an office in the Pentagon that let us go over there and use their machine each month to make the charts.

Those tables have changed format occasionally but continue to be provided to this day, about 25 years later. The Management Information Division continues to send me copies each month. They are now sent on-line rather than in hard copy, and I have filed a copy of each year's information, which I use occasionally.

From 1983 till 1993, long after I had left USDA, I prepared tables of data related to the child nutrition programs which were published twice each year for 10 years in the *School Food Service Research Review* (Hiemstra, 1983-1993). I am not aware of anyone else publishing these data on a routine basis even though they are not confidential.

One of my last serious analyses of the food programs was the subject of a paper called *"Economic Assessment of Recent Developments in the Food Assistance Programs,"* which was prepared in 1983. I presented a summary of this paper at the December meetings of ASSA in San Francisco that December. By then, I had retired from USDA and moved to Purdue University. I sent it off for publication but it was rejected because of its 20-

page length and I was too busy at that time to redraft the paper. I had several requests for copies of the paper, including one from Wendall Primas, a staff person on the House of Representatives' Committee on Ways and Means to whom I sent a copy. The paper was a statistical analysis of the impacts of the major changes in both the child nutrition and FSPs that took place in 1981 and 1982 after the Reagan administration had taken charge and set out to save money by chopping the food programs. Elements of this analysis related to the child nutrition programs were later published in the *School Food Service Research Review.*

*Peru Trip.* In March 1981, I was asked to go to Peru for two weeks to evaluate a pilot FSP that had been operating there. The study was funded by the Agency for International Development (AID), and I was accompanied by a person who was fluent in Spanish even though he knew nothing about food stamps. We stayed at the Hotel Miraflores in the city of Miraflores, a rather nice suburb of Lima. The AID office was located in downtown Lima near the Embassy and an ancient museum that I visited during a break in our meetings, without benefit of my interpreter. It featured some very graphically displayed mummies that impressed me greatly. I was given a tour of the city, and remember hordes of people shopping in the streets with quite rudimentary shops.

After studying their program, which had already been terminated by the time we were there, I explained to them how the program worked in the U.S., and made some recommendations how they could improve their program if they decided to continue it. They had had a very rudimentary way of both issuing and redeeming food stamps. Grocery stores simply passed them through their banking system till they reached their equivalent of our Federal Reserve Bank who paid the stores. There was no attempt at accountability or management of the use of the stamps. Of course, they did not have many funds for administration. I don't believe they ever continued the program. I don't know either if they ever asked AID to cover the cost of the program, which may have been quite reasonable to do.

I certainly enjoyed the trip, however. It was my first trip to Peru and I found it a fascinating place to visit. We met some local people there who seemed to enjoy showing us around. They took us, for example, to one of the large "barrios" on the edge of Lima where thousands of squatters lived on public land in houses made out of paper boxes. Progressively, over time, they would improve their dwellings. There was no running water or sewage system, but every block or two there was a pump over a well that provided water. The people there appeared friendly and nonviolent, but I would not like to visit there after dark. We were taken to Catholic Church where we visited with a priest who was impressed with our interest in their FSP.

The weekend that I was in Peru I decided to go see Machu Pechu, the historic, 500+ year old city on a mountaintop in the Andes, which is very hard to reach. I arranged to take a tour from Lima. I had to take a flight to Cusco, a couple hour's flight south and east from Lima, spend a night there, and then early the next morning catch a train on a narrow-gauge track to Machu Pechu. At Cusco, I met the tour group that I had arranged to join.

At Cusco, we were warned to stay in our hotel for the afternoon, drink coco tea, and rest because of the 11,000 feet elevation of Cusco. But, I could not resist taking a look at the city.

I bought some interesting souvenirs along the street, some Peruvian jade as well as a handmade sweater, and enjoyed visiting with several friendly local inhabitants in my pigeon Spanish. It also had a large, beautiful cathedral that was fantastic considering its age. The cathedral's inside was almost covered with gold leaf.

That evening I suffered severe chills from over exerting myself, but felt fine the next morning. I had breakfast with some reporters and photographers from the National Geographic who were also going to Machu Pechu that day.

Cusco was itself a fascinating place and a center of government. When the Spaniards pillaged the country and were killing local inhabitants, they were—like us—looking for Machu Pechu, but never found it.

Again that evening I developed severe chills from over-exerting myself. It was a long day on the railroad—we spent 5-6 hours, stopping at every village along the way picking up and dropping off local people. It was a great way to see the back-country and the local people of Peru, lots of lamas and a few alpacas along with the farmers. Upon arriving at the foot of the mountain containing Machu Pechu, we were greeted by many local people selling souvenirs and I bought a few. We had to wait for a bus to take us up the mountain for a mile or two to see the city's remains. The architecture of the stone buildings was unbelievably intricate. It is not a large area but very compact. It contained mostly houses but some open areas where people could congregate and shop. It was hard to believe that this city had been constructed by hand. Very little of it had fallen into disrepair. It was a lot of effort, but the trip turned out to be one of the most interesting tours I have ever taken.

The next week, my AID friend and I visited the famous Gold Museum in Lima. I was actually a little disappointed with the artifacts. The gold was mostly in gold leaf form; it was very thin rather than solid-looking gold pieces, and not too impressive to me.

For my return trip to the U.S., I decided to transfer to a flight scheduled to stop at Equitos, Peru deep in the Amazon Forest along the Amazon River. I planned to make a stopover and see the sights before continuing on to the U.S.

That turned out to be a mistake. The secretary at the AID office that made my flight arrangements misunderstood me and thought I wanted to stop at Quito, Ecuador. I did not find out till it was too late to change back. The stopover in Quito was not simple either. I had to stay an extra night there, and was faced with the possibility of spending several days there, due to overbooked flights because it was Easter weekend. Unknown to me, the secretary had put me on a standby flight that had not been confirmed.

I had a pleasant visit in Quito and enjoyed walking around the city. But, that evening I became very ill with Montezuma's Revenge. I had to hunt up a doctor at the hotel to get some medicine. I was staying in a Hilton Hotel, and fortunately they had a doctor. The next day, I bought a beautiful handmade rug made of Lama wool that featured a group of Lamas. I bought it for the equivalent of $7 from some Indians selling rugs in front of the hotel. I had no room left in my luggage so I carried it home under my arm[2]. I was able to get on a flight the next morning, stopping briefly in Panama on the way home.

---

2 I once saw a duplicate of that rug hanging in the reception room of Swift and Company's corporate headquarters in Chicago.

## Other Travel

Other trips that I took during this period included a trip to Atlanta in September 1981 to visit the FNS Southeast Regional Office. I traveled there quite often as I have mentioned, and I had several projects under way down there. This particular trip was to attend a meeting of the State School Lunch Directors. I met with them quite often because of projects we had going with several of them. I got to know them well. In July, I again visited the southeast to attend the annual meetings of the AAEA which was held at Clemson that year. In September, I attended a meeting at Peaks of Otter, which is on Blue Ridge Parkways, south of Skyline Drive. There was a meeting there of S-119, the Southern Regional Research Committee on Demand for Food which I attended each year. One nice thing about this committee was that they had their own budget and paid the member's travel costs to their annual meetings. On that trip, I also went on down to Atlanta and again visited the Regional Office there.

In 1982, I went to Denver in February to attend a meeting of the American School Food Service Association and on the return trip stopped at Kansas State University to visit Allene Vaden editor of the *Research Review*. In July, my wife and I drove to Logan, Utah to again attend the annual meetings of AAEA and stopped at Denver to visit the FNS Regional Office. In November, I went back to Atlanta to attend a meeting there of the WIC state directors.

# A SON'S REFLECTION

By Stephen W. Hiemstra

*M*y father is a quiet man who chooses his words carefully. He is faithful to God, dedicated to his family, passionate about his work, and anxious to have fun. This book is his story written in his own words with a little help from his friends and family.

We do not and will never forget!

## Family Life

My Dad's history, while certainly personal, was also emblematic of his generation.

He was born on April 17, 1931 during the Great Depression. He grew up on a small, feed-livestock farm in southern Iowa and attended college, in part, under the GI Bill.

His education followed a series of apparently serendipitous decisions, which, in fact, allowed the family to prosper during the normally traumatic move from rural to urban employment. Dad was one of the first in his extended family to attend college and our end of the family prospered more than most. God's hand is clearly on him.

Although Dad was one of the first in the Hiemstra family to attend college, he was not the last. Dad firmly believes in education. He made sure that each of his children made it through college and two of us, John and I, have completed doctoral studies. Between Dad, his brother John, my brother John, and I, there are four of us in the extended family with doctoral degrees. We are truly blessed.

## *Professional Work*

Dad worked for the federal government during a formative period, beginning in late Eisenhower Administration through the early Reagan Administration, when belief in the positive contribution that government could make was at an historical peak. President John F. Kennedy set the tone for this golden age of government service in his inaugural address when he chided Americans to: *"ask not what your country can do for you--ask what you can do for your country[1]."*

Dad took up this challenge with vigor and passion. Not only did he strenuously pursue his work writing voluminous numbers of studies and professional papers, Dad was active in professional societies[2] and often took a leadership role and won awards for his work.

Because I followed Dad into a career in agricultural economics, many of the professionals mentioned in this memoir are my own personal friends and colleagues. Early in my career, this posed something of an embarrassment as I worked to distinguish myself from my father. This was a vain effort. Everywhere I went

---

1 http://www.presidency.ucsb.edu/ws/?pid=8032.
2 During his federal service the principal groups were the American Agricultural Economics Association, the American Economic Association, and the Society of Government Economists. During his time at Purdue University, Dad was heavily involved in the International Council of Hotel, Restaurant, and Institutional Educators (CHRIE).

*A Son's Reflection*

at home and abroad, I ran into friends of my father.

During my year abroad studying in Germany, for example, I felt that I had finally escaped the shadow of my father—I was so wrong. One evening, for example, I attended a doctoral celebration party and in the middle of it the department chair walked up to me and invited me to dinner—he apparently knew my father at Berkeley. At another point, I helped a couple of random American tourists order dinner in a restaurant only to learn that the husband was an agricultural economist from Oregon State University and a friend of my father. Another time when a colleague asked if I had authored a journal article in 1963, I joked: *"didn't you know that I am a child prodigy agricultural economist?"* The article was, of course, one of my father's publications.

Now that the need to distinguish my career from my Dad's has subsided it is easier to appreciate the broad scope of his contribution to agricultural economics, particularly in the areas of food consumption, demand, and distribution studies.

## Purdue University

The focus of Dad's writing about his career in this memoir ended with his retirement in 1983 from federal service. This is most unfortunate because, as mentioned in the preface, the years that followed were some of the happiest and most productive years of his working life.

Dad joined the faculty of what is now the School of Hospitality and Tourism Management at Purdue University as associate professor on August 17, 1983. He taught classes such as marketing and strategic management, but also undertook research and consulting for numerous institutes and firms in the hotel and restaurant industries. He traveled, for example, on lengthy study trips to Liberia (Hiemstra 1986) and Hong Kong (Qu & Hiemstra 1994) during these years.

Dad was best known at Purdue University for starting the first doctoral program (anywhere) in the field of hospitality and tourism management in 1989.[1] His first three students—Richard Ghiselli, Joseph Ismail, and Hailin Qu—are now faculty members in their own right. The program that he started now has 30 doctoral students and is a leading program in the field.

Dad was promoted to full professor on August 17, 1987,

---

[1] This was not an easy sell. Critics complained: *why do you need a doctorate to flip hamburgers?*

only four years after joining the faculty. This would be an impressive achievement in any field, but especially so in this case because Dad was entirely new to the field when he joined the faculty. Dad retired on May 17, 1998 and, shortly thereafter, left West Lafayette, Indiana to return to Falls Church, Virginia on the urging of family.

In the fall of 2015 as I prepared to publish these memoirs, I wrote to Barbara Almanza who replaced Dad as director of the graduate program and requested some assistance in assessing Dad's contributions while at Purdue. She assembled a group of faculty members, including Howard Adler, Liping Cai, Richard Ghiselli, Joseph Ismail, Shawn Jang, Xinran Lehto, Doug Nelson, and John Rousselle, to produce an amazing audio CD of remembrances of Dad and his work which the Hiemstra family shared over Christmas. Let me summarize a few observations taken from this hour-long CD.

*Passionate.* Everyone agrees that Dad was passionate about research. He insisted on recruiting the best students and was a stickler for detail. He worked long hours and remained active in professional groups throughout his career. He emphasized quality over quantity in all that he did.

*Caring.* Although Dad cared deeply about his work, he

was equally concerned about the success of his students and about achieving balance between work and play. At one point, for example, Dad audited a class with one of his students and went over homework with him afterwards to help him overcome inhibitions. Dad pushed his students to excel and could be intimidating, but he also knew them well-enough to recognize when their limits had been reached. Dad's nickname among the students was: *"Doc"*. Dad routinely invited students to dinner parties at home and to join him in a round of golf.

*Consistent*. Dad was always well-organized and kept a strict routine. For example, Dad noticed how many pages were used on his color printer (which was available to everyone) and kept track of acquisitions made from the government grants that he oversaw. He also loved his bolo ties—a reminder of consulting that he did for the Navajo Nation while at USDA—and ate the same lunch every day!

*Available*. Dad worked hard but he was always available to fellow faculty members and students. He was a good team player which is obvious from his list of publications because many of his papers are co-authored with both students and colleagues.

## Past Time

*A*s is obvious reading this memoir, Dad loves to travel. Some of my earliest memories were of our semi-annual pilgrimages back to THE FARM. This trip took two days to travel from Washington to Oskaloosa, Iowa (a trip of about a thousand miles) and we normally spent a week in Oskaloosa once we arrived. Often this trip was made in August to take part in the annual Hiemstra family picnic in Pella, Iowa and we almost always visited again at Christmas time. These visits normally included the extended family: Dad's parents, Frank and Gertrude, and the families of his brothers, John and David.

In reading Dad's memoirs, he makes surprisingly little mention of his lifelong love of golf, gardening, bridge, stamp and coin collecting, square dancing, and investing. Like every good Washingtonian, he is an avid follower of political events in the news and he reads both the Washington Post and Wall Street Journal daily.

Also not mentioned in the memoir are our summer excursions to Ocean City, Maryland where even now Dad keeps a condominium at the Marylander as an investment and getaway destination.

### *Faithfulness as a Churchman*

The role of Dad's Christian faith in his life experience has always been important, even if this memoir makes only occasional references. The church has traditionally taught personal disciple, commitment in marriage, and generosity in giving which are all evident in my father's life. Dad was a good role model to the rest of us who benefitted from his faith and devotion to Christ. He also served a number of churches as elder and in other roles.

More than his church work, however, Dad—introduced once as the *"father of the WIC program"*—took seriously the concept that God is the creator of all creation and all knowledge is God's knowledge. His work as an economist was a calling, not just a career. As the Prophet Jeremiah wrote of his own calling:

> *Before I formed you in the womb I knew you, and before you were born I consecrated you; I appointed you a prophet to the nations.* (Jer 1:5 ESV)

Dad's call came early, even before he was aware of it himself. A prophetic call is not necessarily just to preach and teach—we only know of Jeremiah because of his writing. For Jesus' own brother, James, wrote:

> *Religion that is pure and undefiled before God, the Father, is this: to visit orphans and widows in their affliction, and to keep oneself unstained from the*

*world.* (Jas 1:27 ESV)

He was most proud of his contribution to USDA's food and nutrition programs, which provided food to needy families (primarily single moms with kids) to throughout the United States and territories, such as Puerto Rico and Guam, where the need was especially urgent.

Dad, you make us proud.

# REFERENCES

Allin, S., H. Beebout, P. Doyle, and C. Trippe, 1990: "Current Perspectives on Food Stamp Program Participation." In Food Stamp Policy Issues: Results fr om Recent Research, by Mathematica Policy Research, Inc.

Almanza, B. A. 1994. "1994 Update to the Indiana Department of Education Sanitation Videotape Series", (Indiana Department of Education).

Almanza, B. A., and S. J. Hiemstra. 1997. "School Meals Initiative Implementation Manual for Indiana Schools", RHIT No. 97-1 (Indiana Department of Education)

Almanza, B. A., S. J. Hiemstra, and Y.M. Chao. 1994. "Impact of Trash Reducers on Volume of Waste In Indiana Schools", RHIT No. 94-1.

Almanza, B. A., S. J. Hiemstra, and R. Ghiselli. 1993. "Auditing of School Food Service Waste", RHIT No. 93-6 (Indiana Department of Education).

Almanza, B. A., S. J. Hiemstra, and R. Ghiselli. 1993. "Solid Waste Study in Indiana School Food Service Phase II", RHIT No. 93-2 (Indiana Department of Education).

Almanza, B. A., S. J. Hiemstra, and R. Ghiselli. 1992. "An Investigation of School Food Service Waste In Indiana", RHIT No. 92-2 (Indiana Department of Education).

Apt Associates. 1988. Study of the Child Care Program, Final Report submitted to Food Nutrition Service, USDA.

A. T. Kearney, Inc., 1974. Average Commodity Distribution Costs for the School Lunch Program, report prepared under contract with Food and Nutrition Service, USDA.

Beebout, H. 1978. Estimates of Food Stamp Eligibles in July 1978 by State, unpublished report prepared by Mathematica, Inc for Food Nutrition Service, USDA, Oct 4.

California Agricultural Extension Service, Bulletin 786, June, 72 pp.

Choudhury, P. 1975. The Food Distribution System and Food Stamp Program in Puerto Rico, Department of Social Services, Commonwealth of Puerto Rico, report prepared in cooperation with Food and Nutrition Service, USDA.

Choudhury, P. 1977. The Impact of the Food Stamp Program in Puerto Rico, Department of Social Services, Commonwealth of Puerto Rico, report prepared in cooperation with Food and Nutrition Service, USDA.

Choudhury, P. 1978. The Food Stamp Program and Unemployment in Puerto Rico, Department of Social Services, Commonwealth of Puerto Rico, report prepared in cooperation with Food and Nutrition Service, USDA..

Council on Wage and Price Stability. 1979a. Press release, Apr 13.

Council on Wage and Price Stability. 1979b. Pay and Price Standards: A Compendium, June.

Council on Wage and Price Stability. 1980. Second-Year Price Standards: A Compendium, Mar.

Council on Wage and Price Stability. 1981a. History and Accomplishments: Program Years 1 and 2, Food, Agriculture and Trade Division, Executive Office of the President, Jan (100 pages, not published).

Council on Wage and Price Stability. 1981b. Evaluation of the Pay and Price Standards Program. Jan 16.

Council on Wage and Price Stability and U.S. Department of Agriculture. 1979-1980. "Press Release: Monthly Food Price Review," Mar.

Delaney, B. and R. Moffitt. 1990. "Assessing the Dietary Effects of the Food Stamp Program." In Food Stamp Policy Issues: Results from Recent Research, by Mathematica Policy Research, Inc.

Department of Food Science. 1972. Final Report: School Feeding Effectiveness Research Project, New Brunswick: Rutgers: The State University of New Jersey, Jul 1972.

Department of Health, Education, and Welfare. 1970. Ten State Nutrition Survey in the United States, 72-8134, Washington D.C., GPO Pub. No. 72-8134.

Drucker, P.F. 1974. Mangement Tasks, Responsibilities, Practices. New York: Harper & Row.

Economic Research Service. 1963-67. Handbook of Agricultural Charts, annually.

Economic Research Service. 1965. U.S. Food Consumption, Sources of Data and Trends, 1909-63, Edited by S.J. Hiemstra, Statistical Bulletin 364, 194 pp.

Economic Research Service. 1974. The Comparative Costs of Food Purchased by Both the USDA and Local School Systems, 1973-74. Publications Services, Division of Information.

Economic Research Service. Jan 1975-Dec 2002. Agricultural Outlook, AO- I to A0-297, monthly.

Economic Research Service. 1978-2002. National Food Review (Food Review), three times yearly.

Economic Research Service, Feb 2003-04: Amber Waves, published five times yearly.

Edozien, J. C., B. R. Switzer, and R. B. Bryan. 1976. Medical Evaluation of the Special Supplemental Food Program for Women, Infants, and Children (WIC), Department of Nutrition, School of Public Health, Univ. of North Carolina, Chapel Hill, N.C.

Egbert, A. C. and S. J. Hiemstra. 1969. "Shifting Direct Government Payments from Agriculture to Poor People: Impacts on Food Consumption and Farm Income." Agriculture Economics Research 21, 3:61-69, Jul (reprinted as ERS-426).

Evans, R., S. J. Hiemstra, and B. A. Almanza. 1990. "School Commodity Testing, 1989-1990 School Year, Report 1", (Indiana Department of Education).

Fienup, D. F., W. C. Motes, S. J. Hiemstra, and R. L. Laubis. 1963. Economic Effects of U.S. Grades for Lamb, Agricultural Economic Report 25.

Frommer, Arthur. 2007. *Europe on 5 Dollars a Day* (Reproduction of Original Printing).

Head, M. K. and R. J. Weeks, and E. Gibbs. 1973. "Major Nutrients in the Type A Lunch, Analized and Calculated Values of Values of Meals Served." Journal of American Dietetics Association, 23 (Apr).

Florida Department of Education. 1975. Comparison of Type A and Computer-Assisted Nutrient Standard Menus, Food and Nutrition Service, USDA, and Dade County Public Schools. Available from Nutrition Information Center, National Agricultural Library, Beltsville, MD.

Harper, J. M. and G. R. Jansen, 1973. Comparison of Type A and Nutrient Standard Menus in the National School Lunch Program, Phase II report by Agricultural Engineering and Food Science and Nutrition Departments, Colorado State University, unpublished report, Food and Nutrition Service, USDA.

Hiemstra, Michael A. 1990. Hiemstra Family History. Sioux City (unpublished), July.

Hiemstra, S. J. 1966. "Concentration and Competition in the Food Industries," Amrican Journal of Farm Economics, 48:3 Part II: 137-47, Aug. (Awarded $250 price in AFEA essay contest).

Hiemstra, S. J. 1955-57. Iowa Farm Outlook Letter, Iowa State University, (weekly 2-page reports). Editor of about 20 issues and assistant editor of about 80 issues.

Hiemstra, S. J. 1962a. "Concentration and Ownership in Food Manufacturing Industries." MTS, pp 20-27, Aug. (reprinted as ERS-55).

Hiemstra, S. J. 1962b. "Depreciation, A Rising Cost of Processing Food Products," American Journal of Farm Economics, XLIV, 5:1, 577-82, paper presented at annual meetings of the American Farm Economics Association, Storrs Conn., Aug 19-22.

Hiemstra, S. J. 1962c. "Lease-Financing and Returns to Capital of Food Marketing Firms." Agricultural Economic Research, XIV, 1:18-28, published by Economic Research Service, Jan.

Hiemstra, S. J. 1963a. "Profits as a Measure of Profitability," American Journal of Farm. Economics, XLV, 5:1469-73, paper presented at the annual meetings of the American Farm Economics Association , MN, Aug 25-28.

Hiemstra, S. J. 1963b. Rising Depreciation of Assets in Agricultural Marketing Firms, Some Causes and Implications, Agriculture Economic Report No. 47.

Hiemstra, S. J. 1963-69. "Outlook for Food Consumption, Prices and Expenditures." Family Economics Review, Agricultural Research Service, ARS 62-5, reprinted each year from presentations at the Agricultural Outlook Conferences.

Hiemstra, S. J. 1964-66. "U.S. Food Outlook." The Western Hemisphere Agricultural Situation, Economic Research Service, each year.

Hiemstra, S. J. 1968. Food Consumption, Prices and Expenditures, Economic Research Service, Agricultural Economic Report 138, 169 pp.

Hiemstra, S. J. 1969a. "Consumption of Processed Foods in the United States." paper presented at the Centre National Des Exposition Et Concours Agricoles (CENECA) International Symposium, published in Conference Proceedings, Paris.

Hiemstra, S. J. 1969b. "Telescoping 20 Years of Change in the Food We Eat," Food For Us All, 1969 Yearbook of Agriculture, pp. 51-54, U.S. Government Printing Office.

Hiemstra, S. J. 1970. "Food: A Special Issue in Welfare Economics." National Food Situation, NFS-131, Feb.

Hiemstra, S. J. 1978. Evaluation of the Child Nutrition Programs, Part I of Child Nutrition Review, Unpublished report, Food and Nutrition Service.

Hiemstra, S. J. 1975a. "Efficiency and Effectiveness of USDA Food Assistance Programs." paper presented at Food Policy Seminar V, published in Agricultural Food Policy Review: Proceedings of Five Food Policy Seminars, Economics, Statistics, and Cooperative Service, AFPR-2, 109-14, Sept.

Hiemstra, S. J. 1976. "Evaluation of the Food Stamp Program." Proceedings of the American Statistical Association, Paper presented at the national meetings of the American Statistical Association, Boston, MA, Aug 23-26.

Hiemstra, S. J. 1978b. "Proposed Standards for Monitoring the Food Processing Industries." presentation at meeting of the Grocery Manufacturers of America, Madison Hotel, Nov 9.

Hiemstra, S. J. 1978c. Proposed Standards for the Dairy Industry, presentation to representatives of the Milk Industry Foundation, International Club, Washington D.C., Nov 22.

Hiemstra, S. J. 1979. "Cash in Lieu of Commodities in School Food Service Programs." School Food Service Research Review, 3(1):29-32, Fall.

Hiemstra, S. J. 1979. "Economic Importance of the National School Lunch Program." School Foodervice Research Research Review, 1(1);11-14, Summer.

Hiemstra, S. J. 1979a. "President's Anti-Inflation Program as it relates to the Meat Industry,"presentation to the Task Force on Wage and Price Guidelines, American Meat Institute, Crystal City Marriott, Arlington, VA, Jan 18.

Hiemstra, S. J. 1979b. "Agriculture's Relationship to the Anti-Inflation Program." presentation to the Midwinter Conference of the National Association of State Departments of Agriculture, Washington Hotel, Washington, D. C., Feb 6.

Hiemstra, S. J. 1979c. "Should an Inflationary Economy Remain an Uncontrolled Economy." presentation before the 20th Congressional District CommunityConference, "Inflation, the Economy, and You," Riverside Church, NYC, Mar 31.

Hiemstra, S. J. 1979d. "Price Standards and Monitoring of Food and Agriculture." presentation to the National Economists Club, Black Horse Tavern, May 3.

Hiemstra, S. J. 1979e. "Anti-Inflation Program and the Food Industry." Seminar sponsored by Grocery Manufacturers of America, The Greenbrier, White Sulphur Springs, West Virginia, Jun 18.

Hiemstra, S. J. 1979f. "United States' Anti-Inflation Program." Seminar presented to the Economics Department, University of Gottingen, Gottingen, West Germany, Jul 16.

Hiemstra, S. J. 1979g. "Inflation and Foodservice Distributors." Emergency Session on Inflation and Foodservice Distributors, 27th Annual Conference of the Foodservice Organization of Distributors, Hyatt Regency Hotel, Washington, D.C. Sept 16.

Hiemstra, S. J. 1979h. "Inflation and the Food Procession Industry." keynote address to the 5th Annual Convention of the Southeastern Food Canners and Freezers association, Grove Park Inn, Asheville, North Carolina, Oct 26.

Hiemstra, S. J. 1979i. "Impacts of Pay and Price Standards on the Food Industry." paper presented at the Southern Economic Association annual meetings, Atlanta, GA, Nov 8.

Hiemstra, S. J. 1980a. "Structural Implications of the Price Standards of the Anti Inflation Program." panel presentation at Workshop PM-2, "Antitrust Issues in Today's Economy," Nineteenth Annual Conference, the Conference Board, Plaza Hotel, NY, Mar 6.

Hiemstra, S. J. 1980b. "Impacts of the Anti-Inflation Program on Agriculture." presentation at the Washington Farm Convention sponsored by Congressmen Tom Harkins,

Tom Bedell, and Berkley Dashall, Cannon House Office Building, Washington, D.C., Mar 21.

Hiemstra, S. J. 1980c. "Effectiveness of Voluntary Price Standards and their Future Role." lecture presented at the University of Texas at Arlington, Apr 11.

Hiemstra, S. J. 1980d. "The President's Anti-Inflation Program; Standards, Procedures, and Impacts." seminar presented before the Department of Agricultural Economics, Cornell University, Ithaca, NY, Oct 27.

Hiemstra, S. J. 1981b. "Researching Domestic Food Assistance Programs." Proceedings from Perspectives on Food and Agricultural Policy Research Workshop. Farm Foundation, Oak Brook, IL, 134 pp.

Hiemstra, S. J. 1982. "Impacts of Omnibus Budget Reconciliation Act of 1981." School of Foodservice Research Review, 6(2):73-78, Summer.

Hiemstra, S. J. 1983a. "National School Lunch Program Trends." School of Foodservice Research Review, 7(1):6-12, Spring.

Hiemstra, S. J. 1983b. "National Food Policy." The Farm and Food System in Transition, Emerging Policy Issues, edited by Shaffer, Sorenson, and Libby, Michigan State University, Agricultural Experiment Station.

Hiemstra, S. J. 1983c. "Marketing Impacts of the Domestic Food Assistance Programs." Chapter 14 in Future Frontiers in Agriculture Marketing Research, edited by Paul Farris. Iowa State University Press, 1983.

Hiemstra, Stephen J. 1986. Urban food consumption patterns and national food policy in Liberia.

Hiemstra, S. J. 1983-93. "Program Data & Analysis, Summary of Trends." School Food Service Research Review, American School Food Service Association, continuing semiannual series, 7(2: 147-51) Fall, 1983-17 (1:83-88) Spring 1993.

Hiemstra, S. J. and D. B. DeLoach. 1962. Growth Patterns in the Retail Grocery Business,

Hiemstra, S. J. and O. G. Kerchner. 1973. Program Evaluation Status Reports, Studies in Process and IL Completed studies, Office of the Administrator, Food and Nutrition Service, the first in a series of unpublished, semi-annual Economic Research Service, May1963-Aug 1969: National Food Situation, 26 issues, NFS-104- 129, edited quarterly by S. J. Hiemstra.

Hiemstra, S. J., H. C. Boo, D. C. Nelson, and B. A. Almanza, 1998. "School Commodity Testing, 1997-1998 School Year, Report 10", RHIT No. 98-1 (Indiana Department of Education).

Hiemstra, S. J., S. Ham, and B. A. Almanza. 1996. "School Commodity Testing, 1995-1996 School Year, Report 9." RHIT No. 96-3 (Indiana Department of Education).

Hiemstra, S. J., 1993 "Incidence of the Impacts of Room Taxes on the Lodging Industry," Journal of Travel Research, 31(4): 22-26 (Spring).

Hiemstra, S. J., and J. A. Ismail. 1990. "Impacts of Room Taxes on the Lodging Industry," Hospitality Education and Research Journal, 14(2): 231-241.

Hiemstra, S. J., and J. A. Ismail. 1990. Behavioral Models Related to Tourism. In R. Mudambi and T. Baum (eds.), Economic and Management Methods for Tourism and Hospitality Research, Wiley & Sons: London.

Hiemstra, S. J., and J. A. Ismail. 1991. Impacts of Room Taxes on the Lodging Industry: Final Report, prepared for the Research Foundation of the AH&MA, Mar (17 pp).

Hiemstra, S. J., and W. G. Kim. 1995. "Factors Affecting Expenditures for FAFH in Commercial Establishment." Hospitality Research Journal, 19(3), 15-31.

Hiemstra, S. J., D. C. Nelson, and B. A. Almanza. 1993. "School CommodityTesting, 1992-1993 School Year, Report 6." RHIT No. 93-1 (Indiana Department of Education).

Hiemstra, S. J., D. C. Nelson, and B. A. Almanza. 1994. "School Commodity Testing, 1993-1994 School Year, Report 7." RHIT No. 94-2 (Indiana Department of Education).

Hiemstra, S. J., D. C. Nelson, S. Ham, and B. A. Almanza. 1995. "School Commodity Testing, 1994-1995 School Year, Report 8", RHIT No. 95-1 (Indiana Department of Education).

Hiemstra, S. J., P. O'Grady, L. Rondenet, and B. A. Almanza. 1992. "School Commodity Testing, 1991-1992 School Year, Report 5." RHIT No. 92-1 (Indiana Department of Education).

Hiemstra, S. J., N. N. Nadkarni, B. A. Almanza, and C. Sun. 1991. "School Commodity Testing, 1990-1991 School Year, Report 3." (Indiana Department of Education).

Hiemstra, S. J., N. N. Nadkarni, B. A. Almanza, and C. Sun. 1991. "School Commodity Testing, 1990-1991 School Year, Report 4." (Indiana Department of Education).

Hiemstra, S. J. and H. Qu. 1994. Impacts of Food Service Industry on U.S. Agriculture. In H.H. Jensen & J.A. Chalfant (Eds.), Policy Implications for U.S. Agriculture of Changes in Demand for Food. Center for Agricultural and Rural Development, Iowa State University, Ames.

Jordon, M. and M. Matsumoto. 1972. "Impacts of the Food Stamp Program on Three Local Economies—An Input-Output Analysis," Economic Research Service, ERS-503, May.

Johnson, Glenn L. 1986. Research Methology for Economists: Philosophy and Practice. New York: MacMillan.

Kim, W. G., C. Lee, and S. Hiemstra. 2004. The Effects of an Online Virtual Community on Customer Loyalty and Travel Products Purchases, Tourism Management, 25(3), 343-355.

Lane, S. 1974. Effects on Food Expenditures and Levels of Nutritional Achievement of Low Income Households, 1974.

Litschaurer, J. G. 1978. Study to Measure the Impact of Costs and Other Factors on the Quality of Meals Provided under the Summer Program, Phase I, unpublished report.

Litschauer, J. G. and V. A. Canevello. 1977. "Cost Economies of Scale in School Lunch Service." School Foodservice Research Review, 1(1):37-39.

Logan, S. H. and D. B. DeLoach. 1973. The Food Stamp Program: Del Norte and Humboldt Counties, California, California Experiment Station Bull.860, Davis, CA.

Madden, J. P. and M. D. Yoder. 1972. Program Evaluation: Food Stamps and Commodity Distribution in Rural Areas of Central Pennsylvania, Penn State University Bull. 780.

Munger, Robert Royd. 2001. *My Heart, Christ's Home*. Downers Grove: InterVarsity Press.

Nathan, R., F. 1976. "Food Stamps and Welfare Reform," Journal of Policy Analysis, 2:1, Congressional Budget Office, U.S. Congress, 1977: The Food Stamp Program: Income or Food Supplementation, a budget issue paper, Jan 17, 91 pp.

Nelson, P. E. and J. Perrin. 1976. "The Economic Effects of the Food Stamp and School Lunch Programs, fiscal Year 1976." American Journal of Agricultural Economics, Dec.

Nelson, P. E. 1972. "The Michigan Food Stamp Program--A Partial Analysis of Performance." American Journal of Agricultural Economics.

Nelson, P. E. 1978. Food Stamp Redemptions: Their Impact on Food sales by Region, Size, and Kind of Participating Food Stores, Fiscal 1976, Economic, Statistics, and Cooperatives Service (later changed back to ERS), USDA, Agricultural Economic Report No. 410.

Ministry of Agriculture, Puerto Rico. 1974. Consumo de Alimentos en Puerto Rico, 1951/52–1973/74.

National Center for Health Statistics. 1974. Preliminary Findings of the First Health and Nutrition and Health Examination Survey, United States, 1971-72, Dietary Intake and Biochemical Findings, DREW Pub. No. HRA 74-1219-1.

Orshansky, M. 1965. "Counting the Poor: Another Look at the Poverty Profile." Social Security Bulletin, U.S. Dept. of Health, Education, and Welfare (currently Health and Human Services), Jan.

Price, D. W., M. M. Hard, and others. 1976. Evaluation of School Lunch and School Breaifast Programs in the State of Washington, Parts 1 and 2, submitted to Food and Nutrition Service, USDA.

Price, D. W., D. A West, G. E. Scheier, and D. Z. Price. 1979. "Food Delivery Programs and Other Factors Affecting Nutrient Intake of Children," Nutrition and the School Age Child, A collection of readings published by American School Food Service Association, Fall, pp. 32-39.

Qu, H. and S. J. Hiemstra. 1994. Economic Interdependence and Structure of the Foodservice Industry, 1977–1991. Journal of Foodservice Systems, 7(4), 199–216.

Reese, R. B., J. G. Feaster, and G. B. Perkins. 1974. Bonus Stamps and Cash Income Supplements: Their Effectiveness in Expanding the Demand for Food, Marketing Research Report 1034, Economic Research Service, USDA.

Scott, F. E. and S. J. Hiemstra. 1962. "The Food Marketing Industries Recent Changes and Prospects." The Marketing and Transportation Situation (MTS), pp. 15-37, Feb (reprinted as ERS-55).

Stalker, J. C. 1971. Massachusetts Public School Nutrition Survey, Department of Education, Massachusetts.

States, Spring 1965, Report No. 11, U.S. Department of Agriculture.

Sun, C., S. J. Hiemstra, and B. A. Almanza. 1990. "School Commodity Testing, 1989-1990 School Year, Report 2." (Indiana Department of Education).

Supplemental Food Program for Women, Infants, and Children (WIC), Department of Nutrition, School of Public Health, University of North Carolina, Chapel Hill, N.C.

Tennessee Department of Education. 1975. Comparison of Type A and Computer-Assisted Nutrient Standard Menus, Memphis City Schools. Available from Nutrition Information Center, National Agricultural Library, Beltsville, MD.

Unknown author. 1960. The Hiemstra Family History, unpublished.

U. S. Congress. 1946. National School Lunch Act. Washington: U.S. Government Printing Office.

U.S. Congress. 1962. Effects of Federal Lamb and Mutton Grades on Producers and Consumer Prices, Committee Print, 871 Congress, Mar 7.

U.S. Congress. 1964. The Food Stamp Act of 1964, Public Law 88-525, 78 Statistical Bulletin pp. 703-709, Aug 31.

U.S. Congress, 1966. Child Nutrition Act of 1966, P.L, Washington: Government Printing Office.

U.S. Congress. 1970. National School Lunch Act of 1946, Sec. 6 (a) (3) as Amended and Child Nutriton Act of 1966 as Amended, P.L. 91-248, Sec. 3(3)(3), Washington: Government Printing Office.

U.S. Congress. 1971. The Food Stamp Act of 1964, Amendments, P. L. 91-671, 84 Stat., Jan 11 Agricultural Research Service, 1972: Food and Nutrient Intake of Individuals in the United States.

U.S. Congress. 1974. Comprehensive Study of the Child Nutrition Programs. Submitted by the United States Department of Agriculture to the Senate Committee on Agriculture and Forestry, pursuant to Public Law 93-150, Committee Print, 93d congress, 2d Session.

U.S. Congress. 1975a. Food Stamp Program, A Report Submitted in Accordance With Senate Resolution 58, Committee Print, 94th Congress, 1st Session, Senate Committee on Agriculture and Forestry, Washington: Govt. Printing Office, Jul 21.

U.S. Congress. 1975b. Who Gets Food Stamps, Committee Print, 94th Congress, 1st Session, Senate Select Committee on Nutrition and Human Needs, Aug 1.

U.S. Congress. 1977. The Food Stamp Act. House Report 95-464. 95th Congress, 1st Session.

U.S. Government Printing Office. Government Procurement Regulations (A104).

Watts, B. K. and A. L. Merrill. 1963. Composition of Foods, Agricultural Handbook No. 8, Agricultural Research Service.

Waugh, Frederick. 1964. Demand and Price Analysis, USDA Agr. Tech. Bull. 1316.

West, D. A. and R. A. Hoppe. 1973. "Pricing and Participation Rates in the National School Lunch Programs in Washington Public School Districts," Washington State University, Bull.

Westercamp, N. and M. De Jong. 1976. The Hiemstra Family History, Book II, unpublished.

Westercamp, N. and M. De Jong. 1976-1990. The Hiemstra Family History, Book III, unpublished.

Wunderle, R. E. and D. L. Call. 1971. An Evaluation of the Pilot Food Certificate Program in Chicago, Illinois and Bibb County, Georgia, April reports prepared through Oct 1978, with various authors.

# APPENDIX A: FAMILY CHRONOLOGIES

## Brief History of Friesland

The Hiemstra family originated in the Netherlands in the northern province of Friesland[1] where they farmed near the county seat of Leeuwarden which is close to the North Sea.

The Netherlands, which means low-country, refers to the fact that about half the country lies below sea level and consists of land reclaimed from the sea through a system of dykes and waterworks. Late in the Seond World War (1944-45), much of this land was inunddated, having either been destroyed by allied bombings or sabotaged by the retreating German army.

The Netherlands is often mistakenly referred to as Holland, which technically refers only to the two principal provinces of North Holland (which contains Amsterdam) and South Holland (which contains Rotterdam).

The recorded history of the Netherlands dates back to 55 B.C. when Julius Caesar led Roman Legions to establish control over the area. Later in 1701, the War of the Spanish Succession took a heavy toll on the country, as did the wars against Prus-

---

1 See: Hiemstra, M.A., 1990; and Westercamp and De Jong, 1976.

sia and France in the mid-1700s and against Britain in 1780. In 1806, Napoleon took over the country and named his brother, Louis Bonaparte, the ruler of the Netherlands. The Kingdom of Holland was established but lasted only four years at which time Napoleon annexed the region to France. With his defeat in 1813 at Waterloo, near Brussels, the French withdrew. The son of the previous ruler returned from England and took over as King. In 1830, Belgium separated from the Netherlands and the country resumed its earlier growth and development (Hiemstra, M.A., 1990).

The Netherlands are often remembered because of the reformation period, which began in the 16th century. The Canons of Dort (1618-1619), for example, set forth the principles distinguishing Arminism from Calvism, which were later summarized in the acronym, TULIP,[2] which also refers to the most famous flower in the Netherlands. The most famous Dutch painter of this period was Rembrandt who, being influenced by the reformation, painted distinctive pictures of famous passages in the Bible, such as the *Storm on the Sea of Galilee (1633)* and the *Return of the Prodigal Son (1669).*

---

[2] TULIP stands for total depravity, unconditional election, limited atonement, irresistible grace, and the perseverance of the saints.

## Hiemstra Family History

*U*ntil the rule of Napolean, most commoners in Europe had no family name, as was true for members of the Hiemstra family.

My oldest known relative was named Bouwes Andrys, who lived in Murmerwoude, Friesland, was born sometime between 1700 and 1735, and worked as a laborer, according to the records of Leeuwarden. His wife was not identified and, while they may have had other children, his son, Biense Bouwes, is the only one listed in the county records (Hiemstra 1990).

Note that Biense Bouwes took his last name from his father's first name, as was the custom. Similarly, daughters would take their mother's first name as a last name.

Biense Bouwes married Aaltje Pieters on October 10, 1756, in Damwoude where they farmed and they had 11 children. They later moved to Oostrum. Their son, Sytze Bienzes, was bom in Driesum on February 27, 1766 and he married Tetke Feikes on May 29, 1791.

In 1811, Sytze adopted the name, Hiemstra, as a surname for himself and the seven children: Aaltje, Feike, Gryttje, Bienze, Martje, Tjitske, and Romke. This is the first time that the name

Hiemstra appears on the county records.

In 1812, Sytze married a second woman, Trijntj e Renderts Triemstra, who died in 1825 without having had any children.

On July 8, 1826, Sytze married a third time when he was age 60 to Antje Harkes Zuidema, who was born about 1773 in Kooten and only 20 years old when she married. Her parents were Harke Jans Zuidema and Jitske Ennes Boersma. Sytze and Antje had three children, including Feike Sytzes Hiemstra on June 6, 1829, in Oostrum.

Feika (Frank) Sytzes Hiemstra, my great grandfather, emigrated to America in 1853 and settled near Pella, Iowa, only three years after it was founded about 1850. In June 1862, he married Empke De Haan who was born on November 16, 1844, in Friesland and came to America at the age of 3. Together Feika and Empke had nine children:

1. Sytse, born 1863-64,
2. Sytse, born 1865, called Jesse,
3. John F. (August 9, 1867– February 15, 1942)
4. Anna, born 1870,
5. Jette, bon 1873, Hattie, born 1975,
6. Harry, born 1876,
7. Mary, born 1878,
8. Martin, born 1881.

John F. Hiemstra, my grandfather, married Maggie Visser (January 27, 1877–December 20, 1953) on July 4, 1894. She was born on in South Holland, Netherlands to Cornelius and Tuentje Neef Visser who immigrated to America when she was 10 years old. John and Maggie farmed near Otley, Iowa, about 6 miles northwest of Pella, where they lived until retiring to live in Pella in 1931. Together John and Maggie had 11 children:

1. Tillie Henrietta (May 1, 1895–1978)
2. Emma Annette (June 7, 1896–1983)
3. Frank Henry (August 30, 1898–October 4, 2000)
4. Cornelia Jeanetta (October 2, 1900–February 12, 1985)
5. Martin Jesse (November 16, 1902–April 19, 1981)
6. John Cornelius, (March 13, 1905–April 29, 1994)
7. Mary Magdalene (April 2, 1907–September 23, 1974)
8. Nellie Lurana (August 16, 1909– )
9. Margaret Mabel (October 3, 1911–1987)
10. Mabel Kathryn (March 24, 1914–2003)
11. Leona Henrietta (February 27, 1916– )


1. Tillie Henrietta married Sam Poortinga (1885-1981) in 1916. He was born in Friesland. Their first child died in infancy in 1918, but a second child, Marjorie (1919–1990).

2. Emma Annette married John Friezelaar (1892–1923) in 1917. Emma's children with John Friezelaar were Lee Watson (1919-1986) and Joyce La Rae (1923– ). Emma later married John Jan Buwalda (1899–1995) in 1929. His previous children were Sara

and Alice, and together they had a daughter Verna Ruth (1931–2003).

4. Cornelia Jeanetta on December 10, 1920 married Henry Vriezelaar (1896-1972). Their children were Arthur Donald (1920–1987); Madeline Janet (1925– ); John Henry (1928– ); Velma Kathryn (1931– ); Mary Bertha (1933– ); and Coralee Nelle (1936– ).

5. Martin Jesse married Henrietta Rietveld (1904–January 7, 1996) in 1929. Their children were Carl Wayne (1931– ), and Marvin Roy (1939– ).

6. John Cornelius married Lillian Gosselink (1908–2002) in 1931. Their children were Maxine Ruth (1932– ); Donald John (1936– ); Robert Lee (1939– ), and John Dwayne (1944– ).

7. Mary Magdalene married Leonard Gosselink (1905–1991) in 1928. Their children were Charlene Ruth (1928– ); John Stanley (1931–1993); Marjean Mae (1934– ); and Leonard Marvin

(1937– ).

8. Nellie Lurana married Peter Westercamp (1906-1994) in 1933. Their children were Francene Pearl (1935– ); Mildred Joyce (1938– ); Howard Peter (1941– ); and Non 11a Lurana (1945– ).

9. Margaret Mabel in 1935 married Elmer Vogelaar (1907–1982). Their children were Lenora Marilyn (1938– ) and Marcia Ellen (1943– ).

10. Mabel Kathryn married Clifford De Jong (April 21, 1915–June 2 1, 1995) in 1936. Their children were Leo Fred (1938– ); Melba Janice (1940–1995); and Clifford Dale (1943– ).

11. Leona Henrietta married John Ter Louw (1914– 1998) in 1938. Their children were Nancy Ann (1939– ); Marilyn Jean (1942– ), and Andrew John (1946– ).

Frank Henry, my father, married Gertrude Henrietta De Kock (June 30, 1906–April 20, 1999) of Leighton, Iowa on December 17, 1925. Together Frank and Gertrude had three children:

1. John Elmer (June 21, 1928– )
2. Stephen James (April 17, 1931– )
3. David Lee (August 27, 1932–December 8, 1995)

1. My brother, John Elmer, married Norma Lucille Franklin, (1929– ) in 1948. Together they had four daughters:

1. Carol Ann (1955–1986)
2. Ruth Ellen (1957– )
3. Jean Elizabeth (1958– )
4. Nancy Lucille (February 26, 1960– )

1. Carol Ann married Dean Snook, (1957– ) in 1980. Their children were John Landon (1981– ), and Jacquelyn Ella (1983– ).

2. Ruth Ellen married Christopher Schaefer (1959– ) in 1982. They adopted Andrew Franklin (December 26, 1986– ), and Timothy Cody (May 15, 1991– ), both from Korea.

3. Jean Elizabeth married Peter Essler in 1993 but they have as yet no children.

4. Nancy Lucille married Randy Lawson (1955– ) in 1985, but later divorced. Their children were Shawn Walter (1985– ) and

David Randall (1987– ). In 1996, she married Peter Allen Cook and they had one child: Anna Christine (February 17, 1977– ).

3. My brother, David Lee married Sharron JoAnn Johnson (June 8, 1936– ), in 1958. Their only child is Julie Ann (February 1, 1963– ); she married Nicholas Schrum, but later divorced. Their only child is Nicole Ann (March 19, 1997– ). In 2005, she married Timothy Sebetka"

2. I (Stephen James) married Hazel Fern Deacon (October 10, 1930– ) of Guelph, Ontario, Canada on September 13, 1952. Our children are:

1. Stephen Wayne (December 18, 1953– )
2. Diane Sue (April 4, 1956–February 12, 2007)
3. Karen Lee (July 7, 1961– )
4. John David (April 9, 1963– )

1. Stephen Wayne married Maryam Hajatpour (December 18, 1956– ) of Tehran, Iran on November 24, 1984. Their children are:

1. Christine Nousheen (December 14, 1989– )
2. Marjolijn Narsis (April 10, 1991– )
3. Stephen Reza (August 19, 1992– ).

Christine Nousheen married Doug Ferrer on October 22, 2015.

2. Diane Sue married Hugo Brandts (August 18, 1953– ) on November 30, 1980. They adopted a son, William Alexander (January 21, 1991– ), originally of Peru.

3. Karen Lee married Douglas Reed (October 30, 1951– ) on June 2, 1990, but they later divorced. Karen has a son, Alexander James Reed (September 27, 2001– ).

4. John David married Julie Anne Oweis (October 17, 1963– ) on November 25, 1989. Their children are Frank Henry (May 17, 1992– ), Jessica Anne (April 30, 1994– ), John Robert (December 12, 1998– ), and Lauren Nicole (July 23, 2000– ).

## A Brief History of Ede

My mother's family name was named DeKock. One branch of the family originated in the eastern part of the Netherlands, in a village called Ede in the province of Gelderland, near Nijmegen, a few miles from Germany, and close to the Rhine River, which is known to the Dutch as the Waal River. Ede is the location of the Tysseling Mill, a grain mill named after one of my ancesters in the 17th century, which my wife and I visited in 1979 and found the Tysseling initials carved into the supporting structure of the mill (circa 1650).

Nijmegen is known for a battle fought in 1944 to capture three bridges over the Rhine one at Nijmegen and two at neighboring towns which give Allied troops access to Nazi Germany. By the end of four days of intense fighting, 8,000 Americans lost their lives.

The National Liberation Museum in Nijmegen commemorates this battle and is located on one of the landing sites (Groesbeek) for American paratroopers. The movie, *"A Bridge Too Far"* (1977),[1] recounts this battle and the Dutch people marked the 50th anniversary of this battle by issuing a silver coin, which pictures the bridge on one side and paratroopers on the other side.

1 https://en.wikipedia.org/wiki/A_Bridge_Too_Far_(film)

My wife and I visited Nijmegen and the museum in 2005.

## Tysseling, Van Zee, and DeKock Family Histories

My mother's grandmother was a Tysseling whose earliest known relative, Hermanus Tysseling (1729–1802), lived at Ede and was buried near the mill. In 1759, he married Annetje Heynekamp (1737–1810) and they had four children:

1. Hermanus (1760–1833)
2. Geritje (1772–1821)
3. Jan
4. Teunis (1781–1858).

Teunis Tysseling married Teunisje Evers (1787–1858) in 1813 and they had six surviving children:

1. Hermanus (1814–1883)
2. Anthony (1821–1902)
3. Celia (1829–1888)
4. Rijk (1817–1863)
5. Albertus (1825–1844)
6. Gerrit (1833–1933).

Their daughter, Celia, wrote a detailed account of her father's life in Holland and, until he moved to Pella, operation of the mill in Eda. By that time, the mill had been in the family for more than 200 years (out of its total life of about 450 years), but with his departure the mill was retired from operation and it became a national landmark.

Hermanus Tysseling married Hendrika Vander Haar, (1818–1887) in 1844. In 1847, they were among the first to settle in Pella, Iowa and they had seven children:

1. Teunis Albertus (1845–1926)
2. Evert (1847–1918)
3. Teunis (1849–1947)
4. Willem (1852–1934)
5. Arie (1855–1935)
6. Anthonia (1854–1937)
7. Willempje (1857–1866).

Teunis Albertus Tysseling married Egje DeJong (1849–1937) in 1868 and had eight children:

1. Hendrika (1869-1871)
2. Gysbertje (1870– )
3. Hendrika (1871–1903)
4. Peiternella (1873–1876)
5. Wilhelmina (1874–1966)
6. Peter (1877– )
7. Antonia (1880–1901)
8. Hermanus (1883–1944).

Willhelmina, my grandmother, married Stephen S. De

Kock (1869-1953) in 1898 and they had eight children:

1. Engelene Lucille (1898–1979)
2. Agnes Elbertha (1900–1975)
3. Nettie Geraldine (1902–1981)
4. Gertrude Henrietta (June 30, 1906–April 20, 1999)
5. Stephen Gilbert (1910-1996)
6. Gladys Cornelia (1911- 2003)
7. Albert Tysseling (1916- 2004)
8. Eva Mae (1918– ).

1. Engelene Lucille married John Englehoven (1899–1980) in 1921. They had six children: Laura Faye (1922– ), Harley James (1923– ), Virgil Henry (1927– ), Neva Irene (1931–1998), Edna Geraldine (1934– ), and Shirley Ann (1935– ).

2. Agnes Elbertha married John Van Zuuk (1899–1992) in 1922. Their only surviving child was Mary Lois (1923– ).

3. Nettie Geraldine married Cornelius Vroom (1898–1993) in 1923. Their only child was John Lester (January 1925-June 1925).

4. Gertrude Henrietta, my mother, married Frank Hiemstra (August 30, 1898–October 4, 2000) on December 17, 1925 and they had three sons—John Elmer, Stephen James, and David Lee—as

cited earlier in the Hiemstra family history.

5. Stephen Gilbert married Mildred De Reus (1910-2003) in 1934 and they had two children who died the day they were born. They also had a son, Stephen Keith (1943– ), and an adopted daughter, Joyce (1942– ).

6. Gladys Cornelia married Gary Vande Haar (1911–2005) in 1935 and had four children: Phyllis Jeane (1936– ); Arnold (1939-1941), Harold (1942– ), and Richard (1945– ).

7. Albert Tysseling married Janet Kolenbrander (1919– 2002) in 1939 and their children were Marlene (lived 4 days in 1941), Arlan Ray (1942– ), Ronald Dale (1944– ), and Janice Ruth (1948– ).

8. Eva Mae she married Paul Roorda (1915-1998) in 1938 and they had four children: James Philip (1939– ), Herbert Eugene (1943– ), Howard Lee (1949– ), and Alan Wayne (1953– ).

*My* mother's mother's name was Van Zee. In 1847, Engle Van Zee (1775–1868)[1] wrote a chronology of the Van Zee family

[1] His coat of arms consisted of a double eagle on a background of gold.

which includes a photograph of him wearing a top hat and which traces the family back to his grandfather.

Frederik van Zee (1695– ),[2] the grandfather, had ancestors who came from England while his wife's (1693– ) came from Spain. Their children were:

1. Leendert (1718– )
2. Jan (1723– )
3. Govert (1728– )
4. Maaike (1733– )
5. Arie (1735– ).

Govert married Jenneke De Fokert, whose ancestors were driven from Spain for religious reasons in 1522. Their children were: Aaltje (1765– ) and Engle, mentioned above.

Engle van Zee married Engelje Biji (1777– ) and, in 1842, their daughter, Judith (1820–1909), married Stefanus van Zee (1817–1905), whose mother, Cornelia De Kock, had immigrated from France. Judith and Stefanus lived in Herwijnen, in the Province of Gelderland, before coming to America.

Judith and Stefanus van Zee had 11 surviving children,

---

2 Their coat of arms had three red roses.

three born in Holland and 3 in America:

1. Gerrit S. (1842– )
2. Engle (1845–1853)
3. Engeltje Maria (1847–1916)[3]
4. Cornelia Maria (1849–1920)
5. Gjetertje (1851– )
6. Judith (1855–1935)
7. Govert (1858–1941)
8. Gertrude (1861– )
9. Lena (1861– )
10. Jeneke (1862– )
11. Arie (1864–1895).

Engeltje Marie van Zee married Stefanus J. de Kock (1838-1924) in 1867 and they had nine children:

1. Antona S. de Kock (1867–1916)
2. Stephen S. de Kock (1869–1953)
3. Judith de Kock (1872–1937)
4. John F. de Kock (1874–1960)
5. Centinnial de Kock (1876–1878)
6. Art S. de Kock (1879–1939)
7. Cornelia M. de Kock (1882–1917)
8. Rebecca K. de Kock (1884–1961)
9. Harry de Kock (1892–1958).

Stephen S. de Kock, my grandfather, married Willhelmi-

---

[3] Engeltje Maria was the first child born in Pella.

na Tysseling in 1898, as noted earlier.

## Brief History of Pella, Iowa

*I*n 1847, H. P. Scholte, pastor of the Reformed Church, lead between 700 and 800 people to sail in four vessels from Rotterdam and Amsterdam on April 6, 1847 bound ultimately for America. They sailed from the Netherlands to American on the vessel, Peter Floris, with many other families and, during the Atlantic passage, nine people died and three babies were born.[1] They considered going to Texas but decided it was too hot; they also rejected Missouri because slavery was still permitted. Iowa was finally selected because of its frontier location and its good farmland.

Having chosen Iowa, the settlement was named, Pella, which means *"city of refuge"*.[2] Initially, the settlement consisted of just two log cabins. By 1853, they had built Central college which erolled 327 students.

---

[1] Because of religious persecution in the Netherlands and the hardships of the journey, Scholte and his group did not welcome infidels and Roman Catholics in Pella. The prejudice against Catholics was not random, but likely arose because Spain, which ruled the Netherlands harshly for many years (circa 1581 to 1714), was Catholic.

[2] The fourth-century church historian Eusebius of Caesarea tells of the earliest Christians' escape to Pella (in present-day Jordan) from Jerusalem just before the latter city was destroyed by the Romans in 70 A.D.

# APPENDIX B: BIOGRAPHY OF STEPHEN J. HIEMSTRA

Spring 2008 School of hotel and Restaurant Administration

Davis and Lanphere Distinguished Speaker

Dr. Stephen J Hiemstra[1]

Friday April 4, 2008

11:30am-1:30pm in Joe's Room for Graduate Students and Faculty

3:00pm-5:00pm in 203 HESW for Faculty and Graduate Students

    Dr. Stephen Hiemstra is a Professor Emeritus at Purdue University and Senior Research Fellow in the School of Business and Public Policy at George Washington University. He received his Ph.D. in agricultural economics, at University of California, Berkeley in 1960. He is the founder and Director of the hospitality Ph.D. program in the Department of Hospitality and Tourism Management at Purdue University.

    Dr. Hiemstra has 15 years of experience in teaching and research, and 23 years in administration and research at the USDA. His areas of research focused primarily on: 1) supply and

[1] This biography can be found online at: http://humansciences.okstate.edu/chtr/documents/Davis%20Distinguished%20Speaker%20Steve%20Bio.pdf.

demand for lodging services, and impacts of room taxes on the lodging industry; 2) tourism forecasting and impact analysis; 3) foodservice industry structure and demand analysis; and, 4) school foodservice purchasing, pricing, and management. He published over 200 refereed articles including 75 refereed journal articles. He was the recipient of I-CHRIE Lifetime Research Award (John Wiley & Sons) award and the Editor of National Food Situation for 7 years.

His grants and management consulting related to foodservice, lodging, and tourism include: 1) U.S. food assistance program evaluation, management and administration; 2) food marketing economics - e.g. food demand, price analysis, and projections, management information processing and analysis, State Extension Service Agricultural Economist; and 3) U.S. Air Force where he served as communication's officer in Korea.

He has an extensive bibliography of published research, and considerable experience in public speaking and TV and radio presentations, is computer literate, and adept at quantitative statistical analysis.

# APPENDIX C: PLACES LIVED AND CHURCHES ATTENDED

## *Places Lived*

Rural Route 2, Oskloosa, Iowa

Lincoln Way Avenue, Ames, Iowa

643 Pammel Court, Ames, Iowa[1]

Mary Jane Street, Lebanon, Illinois

Fifth Air Force Headquarters at K-55, Oson, Korea

1063 Apartment A Monroe, Albany, California 94706-2283

3704 King Street, Alexandria, Virginia 22302-1905

6808 Trexler Road, Lanham, Maryland 20801

232 Jennings Court, West Lafayette, Indiana 47906

1911 Diplomat Court, Falls Church, Virginia 22043

---

1 http://www.ameshistory.org/exhibits/tribune/10/wf_1008.htm

## Churches Attended

Central Reformed Church, Oskaloosa, Iowa

Collegiate Presbyterian Church, Ames, Iowa

First Presbyterian Church, Berkeley, California

Fairlington Presbyterian Church, Alexandria, VA

Grace Presbyterian Church, Lanham, Maryland

Riverdale Presbyterian Church, Riverdale, Maryland

Covenant Presbyterian Church, West Lafayette, Indiana

Lewinsville Presbyterian Church, McLean Virginia

# APPENDIX D: REFLECTIONS ON A CAREER OF ACCOMPLISHMENTS BY NEIL E. HARL

Through the spring semester of 2016, 314,351 individuals have graduated with Bachelors, Masters and Doctor of Philosophy Degrees from Iowa State University since its founding in 1858. One of these, Dr. Stephen J. Hiemstra, graduated from Iowa State with a B.S. degree in agricultural economics in 1953, an M.S. degree in 1957 also in agricultural economics, and armed with a Ph.D. from the University of California at Berkeley, became a member of the faculty in Purdue University in West Lafayette, Indiana. I knew Dr. Hiemstra in his undergraduate days and I want to share some thoughts about our very similar careers.

As I learned following a family incident a few years back and began writing a memoir of my own, Dr. Hiemstra's life story parallels my own because we both grew up in Southern Iowa during the Great Depression. My father was a tenant farmer whose poor crops in 1934 and 1936 left little for spending on non-essentials. I remember, for example, in October of 1936 when my father told my mother in hushed tones that we had just $100 to get through the winter and put the crops in. At age three,

I did not appreciate just how serious our financial situation was. The extent of our poverty dawned on me later when I realized that I was alone in my class in our one-room, country school during the entire eight years that I studied there.

Dr. Hiemstra and I attended school together during the 1951-52 and 1952-53 academic years at Iowa State University. By contrast, I started in the fall quarter of 1951 and graduated in June of 1955. He switched to agricultural economics while I was in the Department of Agricultural Education as an undergraduate. Although I took several courses in economics and agricultural economics as an undergraduate, I switched to economics as a major in my Ph.D. program. Nevertheless, we studied under some of the same professors.

Dr. Hiemstra lived in FarmHouse fraternity, where he was an active member. I was asked by FarmHouse to pledge shortly after my first quarter at Iowa State, but after a great deal of thought I decided against pledging because of my heavy workload. Although I was fortunate in receiving scholarships, I was working 30 hours per week at the local Hy Vee grocery store, which would prevent me from being a good pledge. Dr. Hiemstra was already a good pledge, being both handsome (which is normally a plus in fraternity circles) and a good student, which was especially important at FarmHouse fraternity. I joined FarmHouse fraternity as an honorary member in 1964, in part, because I became convinced over the years that FarmHouse provided a great environment for its young members.

Dr. Hiemstra and I were also active in Military Science and Tactics (known popularly as ROTC—Reserve Officer Training Corps). In his earlier years he was in artillery but later he switched to Air Force ROTC and went onto active duty with the Air Force.[1] I also started out reluctantly with army artillery, but my enthusiasm grew in my second year and I ended up as a cadet colonel for the 1,350 member Army ROTC group of four battalions in 1954-55. I was offered a regular commission as an officer on graduation, which I declined.

Dr. Hiemstra and I both had breaks in our education after graduation but later returned for graduate school. His break and my own was for two years of military service. After military service, I additionally served a one-year stint as a field editor for the publication, Wallace's Farmer, in 1957-58; I had tried to rent the farm that my father had been tenanting—my first choice of professions at the time—but was unsuccessful. After this break, I came back for three years of law school and then three more

---

1 All physically-able males at universities were subject to the requirement at the time and had to take two years of basic science and tactics in one of the branches of the armed services.

years to obtain a Ph.D. in economics at Iowa State. By contrast, Dr. Hiemstra chose to finish his doctoral studies at the University of California-Berkeley. Our paths did not cross again until we came back later as faculty members, he at Purdue and I at Iowa State.

Thus, Dr. Hiemstra and I shared a common rags-to-riches story made possible by the land grant universities. Both of us started as sons of poor Iowa farmers, but ended up with well-paid professional careers that have, hopefully, made genuine contributions to our communities, our country, and, indeed, the world.

www.ingramcontent.com/pod-product-compliance
Lightning Source LLC
Chambersburg PA
CBHW071726080526
**44588CB00013B/1908**